I0474903

POWER UP

WOMEN CHARGING UP FOR A FULLER LIFE!

Published by: Women of Wisdom, Inc., Davie, Florida
Edited by: Kodiak Communications, Inc., Fort Lauderdale, Florida
Cover Photographs: Tiffany Photography, Fort Lauderdale, Florida

Copyright © 2014
Veronica Ruiz-Ashwal, LMHC, MBA
Elizabeth Lynne Hyatt
Priscilla V. Marotta, Ph.D.

All rights reserved.

ISBN-10: 1493608487
ISBN-13: 9781493608485

Library of Congress Control Number: 2013920441
CreateSpace On-Demand Publishing Services
North Charleston, South Carolina

What successful women are saying about Power Up:

"While the word 'power' may seem foreign to many women, it is the essence of what we unknowingly possess. At Camp Kesem, we continually speak about the ability to empower those around us — the children we serve, the student leaders we train, and the communities we engage. Camp Kesem recognizes and embraces the often-overlooked population of children affected by a parent's cancer. *Power Up* speaks to this new definition of power, and the moral obligation we as women have to claim and use our power for good. The world needs our leadership, so please go out and boldly share your unique gifts!"

Jane Saccaro, CEO
Camp Kesem

"*Power Up* does an excellent job of helping women understand that power is positive and by learning to accept it and nourish it, a woman can generate positive perceptions, emotions, thoughts, words, attitudes, and proactive actions. This book teaches women to embrace their power as a life skill in order to enhance their lives while lifting up and empowering those around them as well. What a phenomenal read!"

Debra Goldman, LCSW
Henderson Student Counseling Services, Director

"*Wow!* What a great topic! This beautifully written book, ***Power Up,*** should be required reading for all women — what a gift these ladies have given us. I can't wait to send one to each of my nieces and the women I care about. This book encourages women to explore and cultivate their own unique Positive Power.

Carolyn Zaumeyer, MSN, ARNP
Nurse Practitioner, Entrepreneur
Women's Awareness
Author, How to Start an Independent Practice

"***Power Up*** captures the key issues facing working women today — their efforts to manage power skillfully while initiating their own management style. The authors are on target with the issues facing all of us. Their solutions are time proven and will resonate with many readers."

Dr. Lenore Alpert, Executive Director
Florida Ocean Alliance

"The authors harness the electric energy within us all and guide women on a journey to that not-so-elusive place of power. They show women that, although breaking through the 'glass ceiling' enlisted the assistance of others, Positive Power truly comes from within and we all have the capacity to generate it."

Cindy S. Vova, J.D., MBA
Family Law Attorney

"Enlightening and motivating. From the first pages of ***Power Up,*** the reader is immediately engaged by thought-provoking statements of gendered power inequality that have existed for generations in society. Boldly presented, power is not something for women to be afraid or ashamed of, but a tool to readily embrace. ***Power Up*** gives women invaluable information and guidance to help change mindsets concerning the negative connotations of power."

Pamela Galan, R.N., MPA, Chief Operation Officer
Henderson Behavioral Health, Inc.

"After reading the book, I was able to understand and clarify the difference between control vs. power and not to be afraid of it. It made me realize that I tend to take the perspective of being powerful in many areas without realizing it. The authors helped me understand the many aspects of being powerful and gave me tools to use for years to come."

Anita Blickensderfer
Entrepreneur

"*Power Up* offers a roadmap for becoming more aware and acting through our power to be at our best in our love, personal, and professional relationships. Ms. Ruiz-Ashwal, Ms. Hyatt, and Dr. Marotta remind us that accepting our power and acting through the framework of "power within" allows us to be at our personal best for ourselves and for others."

Kathy D. Geller, Ph.D.
Assistant Clinical Professor
Educational Leadership and Management
Drexel University

"After reading this book, I feel empowered to take on the world, inspire other women, and achieve all of my goals and aspirations within my college community and my future profession. I CAN and WILL do anything I set my mind to."

Kelsea Grant, Student
Co-director of Camp Kesem
University of Florida

"This book ratifies the real meaning of power. *Power Up* tells you why women's leadership is the key to the world's transformation. As an Editor, I am passionate about what I am doing and the impact we make to the communities we call a 'melting pot'. To promote understanding within different cultures is to promote peace in the world."

Evelyn Alcala, Editor
Ciudad Weston Newspaper

"As a business owner, mother, and wife, the authors' interpretation of how power is often perceived rang true to me. I particularly enjoyed their suggestion that power is a skill that can be developed. I can personally attest to how necessary it is for women to channel power into all aspects of our life. A must read for women seeking success in all areas of their lives!"

Lana Kerr, Owner
Fat Loss Coach Wellness Clinics

"As I entered into the field of technology in the 1980s I found I was often the only woman in a meeting and the only woman in a managerial position in my organization. Managerial women need Positive Power skills to effectively create a productive corporate culture. *Power Up* gives you essential skills to manage successfully."

Sharon Grover-Renda
Director of Compliance

"Positive Power lessons are wonderful tools to build a quality life."

Judith L. Coughlin, Ph.D.
Program Professor,
Nova Southeastern University

"Three generations of women's voices unite in shaping this timely book that describes the constructive use of personal power and how it can enhance, enrich, and exalt a woman's personal life, professional career, as well as all relationships. Framed within a historical, cultural, and psychological context, Dr. Marotta, a Baby Boomer, Veronica Ruiz-Ashwal, of Generation X, and Elizabeth Hyatt, a Millennial, systematically detail how societal changes, emotional transformations, and cognitive awakenings create opportunities for women to embrace their true potential.

Dr. Andrea Corn, Psychologist
Co-author, Raising Your Game

Veronica Ruiz-Ashwal, LMHC, MBA

To my beloved parents, Manuel Ruiz and Magda Arce
Your love, support, and understanding have made all
my achievements possible.

To my wonderful sister, Silvia Ruiz
You always are by my side, guiding me on my path,
no matter where I go and what I do.

To my husband, Ira Ashwal
Thank you for all your love, patience, and encouragement.

To my dear son, Joseph Ashwal
You bless our home with love and give our lives so much meaning.

To Dr. Priscilla Marotta
Thank you for seeing in me what I did not see in myself,
and for pushing me to greater limits.

To all my friends
You have been here with me through tough moments
and have helped me — way beyond my expectations — to never give up
and to keep going.

To our editor Dee Moustakas
Thank you for helping blend our literary styles.

To my patients
You trust me in your lives and allow me to remind you that your
dreams should stay big and your worries small.

Elizabeth Hyatt

To my mentor, Dr. Priscilla Marotta
You taught me invaluable wisdom: Women are powerful,
not powerless.

To my parents, Karen Myatt and Steven Hyatt
You established my family values, invested in my education,
and provided political debates around every dinner table.

To my brother, William Hyatt
Your carefree spirit provides much needed humor
and joy to my life.

**To my mother and grandmother, deceased,
Margaret Hyatt and Lynne Bello**
The past has shaped who I am.
Your legacies will continue to impact my life.

To my grandparents, Donald and Irene Hyatt
Your support of my education has given me tools
to live a successful and fulfilling life.

To Dee Moustakas, our editor
Thanks for helping my writing flow.

To my Sisters of the Heart
Sharing adolescence and adulthood together sparked my voice
for this book.

Priscilla V. Marotta, Ph.D.

To my beloved, deceased parents Fleurdelis and Joseph Marotta
You gave me permission to be powerful and be "out of the box."

To my, deceased godparents, Violanda and Lawerence DiVenuti
You celebrated my accomplishments and encouraged my dreams.

To my husband, Robert MacDonald
You challenge my thinking, support my multiple projects,
and add joy to my life.

To my beloved son, Christopher Joseph Fiore Marotta, Esq.
You teach me to be humble, add love to my life,
and you are an impressive man.

To my Co-Mom, Beth Fiore
You are an exceptional woman.
We have a special bond and a special son.

To my Mentoree, Elizabeth Hyatt
You personify the intelligence and ambition of a future generation
of exceptional women.

To Veronica Ruiz-Ashwal, LMHC, MBA
Your leadership at the Center of Psychological Effectiveness is
outstanding.

Priscilla V. Marotta, Ph.D.

To my cousin, Linda King Parker
You were the patient listener who brought a new dimension
to Positive Power.

To my network of professional women
Each of you has encouraged me each step of my career.
You are role models and outstanding resources.
Heartfelt thanks for the powerful support you add to my life.
Special thanks to the Women's Executive Club.

To our editor, Dee Moustakas, who is part of my sisterhood circle
Your patience and exceptional skills contributed greatly to this book.

To my patients
You invite me into your lives and give me an invaluable
window into the struggles of living.

TABLE OF CONTENTS

Chapter 5 Advanced Power Robbers Awareness

Chapter 6 Charging It Up: Advanced Positive Power Lessons

Chapter 7 The Talents of Women

Foreword

Self-help books for women run the gamut — from telling us to talk, dress, and think like men to sublimating our intuition, nurturing side, and collaborative nature to get ahead personally and professionally. Well, not this book! This book delivers a powerful message about having it all, including a life you love, and presents it from the perspective of three generations.

To Baby Boomers: You are the heroines. Your generation paved paths to boardrooms, women-owned businesses like mine and all the way to the Supreme Court. Your courage and wisdom, and, yes, your struggles created the consciousness that women can do whatever they set their minds to. As you read this book, you'll recognize the hard-won lessons of the '60s and '70s, and realize how many legacies you left and Positive Power tools you mastered. I am proud to stand among you.

To Gen Xers: You are in the middle. You benefit from the progress of previous generations and from the changing attitudes of society toward women on the world stage and in the global marketplace. This book identifies the power drains women face, and provides specific counter measures to thwart them. Read the case studies to understand how women unknowingly sabotage themselves because of gender-based messages they received as girls. Realizing what robs you of your power puts you in a better position to succeed.

To Millennials: You are on the cutting edge. You have a world of timesaving technology at your fingertips and enough brainpower, energy, and enthusiasm to tackle almost any task. One of your greatest assets is your supreme confidence. Use this book as your career/life GPS. Take advantage of the strides made years ago, and set an example for those who come next.

Maybe if I had followed my passion for baking instead of finance, I would have known years earlier the joy of putting my feet on the floor each morning. Even as I received my first purchase order via fax in 1994 for pallets of brownies, my mother's words echoed in my head: "So when are you going to get a real job." See, to my mother a nine-to-five job working for an established, man-owned company was safe. She didn't have to worry about me. To her, a steady paycheck was best. Making waves — trying something no one had done before — was scary.

Thanks to the encouragement of my "sisters of the heart" and my own tenacity I now have the opportunity to put a smile on millions of faces every day, support worthy causes, and sleep well at night knowing I have accomplished something that was once only a dream.

Sheila G. Mains
Founder/CEO
Sheila G's The Original Brownie Brittle Company®

Executive Profile
Sheila G. Mains — A Genius in the Baking

Sheila G. Mains started her booming brownie company in 1992 after losing her CFO position with an industrial advertising agency. Refusing to be just another Friday afternoon casualty, she embarked on her "Plan B (Brownie)."

Armed with her passion for sweet treats and scrumptious samples, Sheila began selling her brownies to local corporations and retail stores. In 1994, Sheila's brownies were discovered by one of the executive chefs at a major theme park, and she became an overnight success.

When the economy took a downturn in 2009, Sheila found herself in need of another "Plan B (Brownie)" or in this case "Plan BB (Brownie Brittle)." Americans were no longer saving money for their next theme park vacation; instead, they were trying to save their homes. So, Sheila took her love of the crisp brownie edges to market, and the rest is history.

Launched in its current packaging in April 2011, Sheila G's Original Brownie Brittle snack has been available on thousands of store shelves in the U.S., Canada, Mexico, Australia, Korea, and the Caribbean. Brownie Brittle has been decorated with numerous awards, including "Best New Snack Product of 2012" from the National Confectionery Sales Association of America and was a finalist in the Sweets & Snacks Expo's 2012 "Most Innovative Products Award."

In best-selling Chocolate Chip, Mint Chocolate Chip, Salted Caramel and Toffee Crunch flavors, Brownie Brittle snacks are available at major retailers or online at BrownieBrittle.com.

Brownie Brittle partners with The Weinstein Co. to provide snacks for movie premieres, as well as their Golden Globe and Oscar events. The company also partners with Cookies For Kids' Cancer, providing product and profits to help fund pediatric cancer research.

Introduction

"Do not wait for power to be offered."

— Sheryl Sandberg,
Author, COO, Facebook

Welcome to three generations of authors' viewpoints. The three of us are role models for sisterhood that extends beyond generations. Dr. Priscilla V. Marotta is a licensed psychologist and the founder of the Center of Psychological Effectiveness. Veronica Ruiz-Ashwal, LMHC, MBA, is a licensed therapist and the owner and President of the Center. Elizabeth Hyatt has been a staff member at the Center since she was 15. She consistently makes significant contributions to the Center's social media and marketing program and is the editor of our online newsletter. She has demonstrated the wisdom of youth by valuing women role models from other generations.

Inspired by Sheryl Sandberg's book *Lean In*, we all strongly agree that the reason women do not *lean in* is their discomfort with power. This book is dedicated to increasing your comfort with power and helping you develop power tools. We coined three terms to illustrate some of the essential ingredients of power: *healthy-selfish*, *Positive Power*, and *mindercise*. We hope these concepts speak to you strongly enough that you incorporate them into your daily life.

BABY BOOMER: Priscilla V. Marotta, Ph.D.

I remember the consciousness-raising groups of the '60s and '70s. The feminist movement helped propel me back to doctoral studies in psychology at 35, having a son, Christopher, at 40, and opening the Center of Psychological Effectiveness at 43. It is exciting to have 2014 be the twenty-fifth year of the Center providing psychological services to the community. My first book, *Power and Wisdom: The New Path for Women*, was published in 1999 and recognized by the Florida Psychological Association with the "What a Woman" award. This book raises Positive Power concepts to a new level.

Successfully navigating through life and activating your Positive Power requires that you have "sisterhood advocates" or "women of the heart." Sisterhood advocates are mentors, cheerleaders, truth tellers.

They recognize your strengths and encourage you to maximize your talents. Sisterhood advocates are also fun to have around.

Women sometimes undermine other women. This is an unfortunate reality. So, be careful when assessing who would be a sincere sisterhood advocate for you. Gender alone does not determine supportiveness. Regrettably, there are many women, who despite being raised in the new millennium, do not understand the value of woman-to-woman sisterhood. A realistic number of sister advocates to have is four.

Mentoring relationships are essential to healthy living especially for younger women, because they benefit from the direction and wisdom offered by older generations. These relationships positively affect both the mentor and the mentee, building upon communication, leadership, and power skills.

Women of the heart add extreme value to your life. They are trustworthy, help you decrease stress, and problem solve life's challenges. They keep you moving toward your life goals even during dark, discouraging times. Treasure your sisterhood advocates. They are the ones who help you live your life to the fullest.

GENERATION X: Veronica Ruiz-Ashwal, LMHC, MBA

As I started my journey in Peru, I never could have predicted the course my career and personal life in the United States would take. I was always open to new opportunities and not afraid to take risks. I, like many members of my generation, do not think of having limits. I saw no conflict among marriage, career, and motherhood. I treasure all aspects of my varied life. This book is dedicated to "having it all." However, "having it all" requires setting realistic standards and clear boundaries, and minimizing guilt with healthy-selfish behaviors. Women can "have it all" by activating the Positive Power tools we share with you throughout this book.

Careers should not be a temporary part of a woman's life until she has children. Both parents need to share child-rearing responsibilities.

Many patients at the Center stopped their careers to raise their family, only to find themselves divorced and permanently off the partnership, CEO track.

Activate your Positive Power tools to set the boundaries you need and to make discriminating life choices. Decide what's necessary and what satisfies you the most. Cut or delegate activities you don't enjoy or can't handle. Remember that it's OK to respectfully say "no." When you quit doing the things you do only out of guilt or a false sense of obligation, you make more room in your life for the activities that are meaningful to you. Make a conscious decision to separate work time from personal time. When you're with your family, for instance, turn off your cell phone and put away your laptop. Schedule family events on a calendar, and keep a daily to-do list. Do what needs to be done, and let the rest go. Limit time-consuming misunderstandings by communicating clearly and listening carefully.

The most essential self-care behavior, in addition to mindercise, is physical exercise and healthy eating. Our bodies need to stay strong and healthy in order to enjoy all our "buckets of pleasure." Nurture yourself by eating healthy foods, include physical activity in your daily routine, and get enough sleep. Set aside time each day for an activity you enjoy. Remember, striking a healthy balance can be a challenge, but it's worth the effort.

Also, women need to be realistic: the world is highly visual. Psychological research reports that attractive and physically fit people consistently get more opportunities. Recognize that you are a brand. Each day, you sell yourself by the way you present yourself in public. This is not about women being sex objects with cleavage and large breasts. It's about you defining your own style.

Wear clothes that make you feel good. When you feel and look good, you exude confidence. Find time to study your body type and wear clothes that complement it. Don't force yourself into tight-fitting clothes if you know they only make you feel uncomfortable. Read some of the many books, magazines, and online articles available about finding the best fit for your body type.

Create your own style. What's so wonderful about the 21st century is that you do not need to conform to trends. You can wear anything that makes you happy and comfortable — and still be stylish. You just need to figure out what style suits you best. Do tailored clothes match your personality? Do you want to blend in or stand out?

Are you the classic type? Athletic? Do you want to have the relaxed I-work-at-home look? Experiment until you find a look that feels right. Then make it your signature style.

Creating your own brand is important. It can change and evolve over time, but remember every time you walk out the door, you make a statement. Be sure yours is powerful!

MILLENNIAL: Elizabeth Hyatt, University of Florida senior, concurrently enrolled in Political Campaigning master's program.

When my stepmother, attorney Karen Myatt, introduced me to Dr. Marotta, who could have foreseen where it would lead? My part-time job at 15, evolved six years later into being invited to co-author this book. The power skills I learned over the years from Dr. Marotta and at the Center helped me cope with the death of my mother from cancer, my father's survival from cancer, and the challenges of college.

As we researched the concepts for this book, I became aware of how few of the women in my generation give any thought to the role of power in their lives. I worry that my generation takes the advances women have made for granted. My research included a 2012 study from the Bentley University Center for Women and Business noting that a significant percentage of millennial women had FEWER aspirations for leadership than men. This is a troubling finding. The world needs talented, powerful women in leadership roles. I hope this book sparks the power conversation for my generation.

Women *can* have it all. In today's world, women can have careers, families, significant others and as many sources of pleasure as possible. If we think of life as a balance scale where problems will always find us, it is essential that we consciously ensure positive experiences balance the scale. Our lives require different sources of pleasure, including a career. Women who elect not to have careers deprive themselves of a significant source of pleasure and growth.

As a university student, my classes are filled with intelligent, articulate, driven women. The majority of my classmates are women, and yet, the number of degreed women entering the workforce does not reflect the number of women receiving an education. We educate our young women, but they do not stay in the game. They compromise their years of hard work and dedication for others. This is not powerful behavior.

Many of my female college classmates joke about pursuing their "MRS" degree. Their intention is to dedicate their time and energy to finding a husband not getting an education. The prevalent perception is that to be a good mother you have to put your career on hold. In the words of Dr. Marotta, "women need to be the cake, and children and men are the icing." The Power Up message is take full responsibility for all aspects of your life.

Thirty years ago the term "work-life balance" wouldn't have crept into everyday conversation. However, as the workforce has grown, shrunk, and changed on a variety of levels, this term has elbowed its way into the new millennium. It describes a concept a lot of people are trying to achieve. There was a time when the boundaries between work and home were fairly clear. Today, however, with cell phones, tablets, laptops, work is likely to invade your personal life. Particularly for my generation, we are always connected with technology and this will be a challenge. It is, however, a challenge we must face. Still, work-life balance isn't out of reach. Evaluate your relationship to work. Keep in mind that balance does not necessarily mean equal. Rather, it's a balance that enables you to work and live life to its fullest, with the least amount of stress.

I hope my generation continues to build on the foundation of opportunity created by prior generations and that they remain in the game and leverage their careers to positions of leadership. The challenge for

Millennials is to set higher goals and keep the momentum going for the advancement of the talents of women. Let's start the conversation!

POSITIVE POWER TIPS

We hope, as you turn each page, that Positive Power tools become part of your repertoire. Living your life to the fullest means living a life you love. To quote celebrated English author, Rose Tremain, "Life is not a dress rehearsal." You only have one life to live, so you need to make it count.

We encourage you to carefully read both the beginning and the advanced power robbers. Remember these insidious thieves can drain your life and pull you off track. You cannot eliminate power robbers — you have to manage them. We recommend that you write out the counter thoughts for the power robbers most relevant to you. Then read them out loud. Reading them and hearing them helps encode them from your short-term memory to your long-term memory.

We believe you create your own destiny. Your thoughts and your beliefs control both your feelings and your actions. Your feelings are not a virus you catch in the air. Your feelings come from your thoughts. Review our power lessons. Repeat the affirmations. Think powerful thoughts, and powerful behaviors will result.

We send our heartfelt wishes, and hope in some small way, this book enhances your life. Refer to it often, like you would a user manual. Now, power up, and charge your life to the fullest!

1

Power is Not
a Dirty Word

*"Power is strength and the ability to see yourself
through your own eyes and not through the eyes of another.
It is being able to place a circle of power at your own feet
and not take power from someone else's circle."*

— Lynn V. Andrews, Author

Power and Women

Confusion With Power

Power and women — the phrase rings strangely in our ears. Powerful people mainly have been men. Throughout the centuries, women have been characterized as weak, passive, and dependent — at the opposite end of the spectrum from the aggressive strengths attributed to men. It is a disservice to both women and men to identify men as powerful and strong while classifying women as passive and weak. To live a psychologically healthy life, men need to be able to express their feelings, demonstrate caring, and display vulnerability. Likewise, women need to exert leadership, mobilize to meet their needs, and manage their lives.

Research studies show that gender characteristics are largely a product of socialization. As women and men grow up, dozens of cultural messages are communicated regarding female and male behaviors. Messages for women have been: be accommodating, considerate, nurturing, and demure. Only now are cultural messages beginning to communicate women's use of power. Naomi Wolf discussed in *Fire With Fire* the need for women to be socialized with a different message to recognize and use their power. Wolf notes that women have enormous unclaimed power, and states, "Women are far more powerful than they know, have far more leverage than they are using, and can raise their voices to make rapid, sweeping, irrefutable changes in the conditions of their lives." Sheryl Sandberg in *Lean In* exhorts women to strategically leverage their talents to leadership positions.

Clearly, in both psychological research and mainstream literature, momentum is building for women to be socialized with a new message — one that advocates equipping themselves with a set of power tools. This book is a retraining manual for women. It differs from other perspectives by encouraging women to create a new *perception* of power. As a concept, power often becomes confused with control, and has been misused and distorted over the years. In *The Psychology of*

Women Quarterly, Lynn R. Offerman, Ph.D., noted, "Models of female achievement need to be more complex than models of male achievement, because women leaders reflect a blending of the traditionally male achievement profile with the uniquely female perspective."

Our goal is that, after reading this book, you will understand that power is a skill, like any other, for achieving goals. You will learn that to be effective you have to use power to put your beliefs and needs into operation. You'll discover you need power to advance your own development — and not to limit the development of others. You'll realize once you shed your lifelong conditioning that power is to be avoided you'll move to an understanding that power is essential to effective living. Power pervades every aspect of our lives, and is a creative force to be embraced. We ask that you have an open mind and a readiness to acquire power skills. So, let's get started!

Power — What Is It?

Power is a word that has multiple meanings. Unfortunately, many of the meanings are shaded by images of domination and hurtfulness. Power has been contaminated by negative images of bulldozing or controlling others. The positive use of power requires one to separate the concept of power from the contamination of societal meanings. You cannot integrate power into your life without first wiping your mind clear of any preconceived ideas about power. But how do you start? The following exercise enables you to identify your "power blocks." Sit down with a blank piece of paper, and write the word POWER in large letters. Next, write down all the words, feelings, and phrases you associate with power. The words you associate with a negative connation are your personal "power blocks."

Imagine for a moment that you are hearing the word power for the first time. Open your mind and your heart to understanding the concept of power from a perspective you have never before held. Power requires increased study and understanding due to the lack of a consistent definition. Furthermore, psychologists often talk about the power process without using the word power, and often have obscured the role power skills play in our lives.

Webster's Unabridged Dictionary has thirty-two definitions for power. It states that power is the "ability to do or act; capability of doing or accomplishing something, ...great or marked ability to do or act; strength; might; ...a person or thing that possesses or exercises authority or influence, ...energy, force, or momentum, ...to inspire; spur; sustain." Power is the ability to achieve, to expend energy; it is the force for bringing inspiration to others, and is central to being effective in life. Power is the key to personal achievement. One cannot be effective in life unless one is powerful.

Power is also a necessary part of living and loving. Acting with confidence, having control over your life — this is use of power — and it exists whenever two people interact in any setting. Just be sure not to confuse power with physical strength or force. Rather, it is **the energy you emit to achieve goals.**

Frequently, love is defined as the exchange of personal power to enhance the nurturing of both individuals. However, when it comes to love, women need to make an important mind shift so they see power is *really* the foundation of healthy love. Using power increases your "love quotient." Oftentimes, women equate being powerful with being "unlovable"; when in fact, the opposite is true! A powerful **YOU** has thoughts, feelings, and accomplishments to share. Being a powerful person not only enhances your love life, it enables you to survive. Power is reassuring to the conscious mind and releases endorphins into your body.

And, we all know the release of endorphins is essential to mental and physical health, as well as a sound immune system. Several studies have demonstrated that the use of personal power has a positive influence on the health of the body. Research studies report that 60 percent of visits to physicians are by the "worried well." The relationship between psychological factors and physical health has been demonstrated in heart disease, gastrointestinal difficulties, and cancer, among others; this relationship even extends to studies on aging. A case can be made that using power enhances longevity. **Thus, power enhances the mind's immune system and leads to healthier lives.**

Exerting your power in romantic relationships is crucial to the health of the relationship. The four cornerstones of a healthy, romantic relationship are communication, respect, trust, and compatible sexual interactions. Effective respect, trust, and communication come from your lover viewing you as someone who is capable and competent. Acquiring skills of capability and competency require the use of personal power. Inadequate use of personal power can undermine a romantic relationship. The following clinical case provides an example of how power anorexia — the inability to use power — eroded a marriage.

Julie's Story

Julie is an attractive woman — 34, tall, well groomed — employed in a managerial position for a national company. She sought therapy after her second divorce. During initial sessions, Julie was tearful, had difficulty expressing her feelings, and felt abandoned by both former spouses. Her husbands had been well-educated men, with financially stable jobs, and both had been initially loving and caring in the relationship. During therapy sessions, a clear pattern began to emerge. Julie was an insecure woman who questioned her self-worth, needed a great deal of reassurance, and questioned her former spouses constantly on their commitment to the relationship. Her second husband still maintained contact with Julie, and agreed to attend a session.

During the session, her former spouse, Tom, discussed at length his initial love and commitment to Julie. Tom shared that he had been worn down by Julie's childlike behaviors over their six-year marriage and her need for constant attention and reassurance. He had reached the conclusion that Julie was unable to be a life partner. Tom stated, "In future relationships, I want a woman who is in touch with her personal strengths and is able to be a powerful person, able to be a partner." Julie's case demonstrates that having a strong sense of self-worth, clearly communicating your needs, and being a person who uses power results in mutual respect, mutual trust, and a partnership relationship. Powerful behaviors enhance romantic attractiveness — contrary to the myth that weakness adds to the desirability of the female. In actuality, personal strength and power increase the romantic allure for women and men alike.

Necessity of Power

Too often, women and power are seen as contradictory. There's the tendency to label a powerful woman with the "B" word. Women need to reject this stereotype, because it causes them to bypass opportunities and avoid constructive confrontation. Women need to recognize that being true to our goals and our talents is essential to living a fulfilling, happy life. Just as a boat cannot reach its destination without power, you, too, need power to navigate through life's unpredictable waters. We're here to show you how to use power with comfort and embrace it as one of life's necessities.

2

Positive Power

*"I am a woman in process. I'm just trying like everybody else.
I try to take every conflict, every experience,
and learn from it. Life is never dull."*

— Oprah Winfrey, Entrepreneur

Embracing Positive Power

Are you ready to embrace a new perception of power? If there is a reason women fail to "lean in" as noted by Sheryl Sandberg, COO of Facebook, it is because they have not embraced power. You have taken the time to purchase this book, now take the time to embrace the concept of Positive Power.. Allow your mind to develop a new openness and a new template for power.

Power is Feminine

Power is the ability to take action and engage in effective living. Neither men nor women own power. As the human species evolved, men were associated with physical power in their role as hunters seeking food. This survival trait of using male physical strength caused power to be associated with men. Yet physical power is a very small dimension of the concept of power. Even in *Webster's* definition, physical power ranks fifteenth on the list.

As Western civilization evolved, male behaviors became the benchmarks for desirable social behaviors. The social phenomenon of viewing male behaviors as "ideal" and female behaviors as "other" is called androcentrism. This separation has imposed limitations on individuals and subsequently on society. Male and female behaviors are both valuable and essential to society and quality of life. Also, individuals cannot be explained or defined solely by their gender. All of us embody a unique combination of skills, talents, and behaviors. Unfortunately, history, theory, and popular conceptions about power have not included or addressed women's experiences.

The assertiveness movement of the 1970s presented a strategy for women, but it lacked one crucial element: a direct power-training program. Assertiveness training encouraged women to express their needs and be more vocal — to assert themselves. However, rather than foster empowerment, the subtle message was for women to "be appropriate" and "nice" in the expression of their new skills. Once again, women were deterred from being powerful. Women need to understand and redefine power, not be excluded or discouraged from power use by verbal semantics.

Early in Western civilization, social stereotypes of women and men emerged. The difficulty with all stereotypes is that polarity thinking arises. Polarity thinking is black or white — all-or-nothing thinking. It assumes the presence of opposites. In reality, human beings operate on a continuum. A continuum of behaviors exists with opposites being useful only as contrast points. Few human beings exist at one or the other end of the spectrum. The majority of human beings are found somewhere on the continuum between the two points. Thus, polarity thinking does a disservice to both men and women. However, gender stereotypes and polarity thinking are still present today. The stereotype is that men are powerful and women are thoughtful; men are leaders and women are team players.

Often, women, as they consider power behaviors, find it difficult to overcome past stereotypic images. Thinking is a complex process. We make sense of information that surrounds us by imposing some mental order on it. Breaking stereotypes means reconsidering the mental order you've assigned. The cognitive framework or schema that one places around a concept is essential, and for a stereotype to be modified, new ideas have to be learned, especially the concept of power. Problematically, highly valued feminine traits are warmth, expressiveness, peacemaking, giving, nurturing, thoughtfulness, accommodating, emotional, and gentleness. Although women possess these traits, it does not preclude them from using these traits with power. Power can no longer be built only into the framework of male behavior. Power, as a cognitive framework, needs also to be incorporated into the female mindset.

Regardless of achievements, many women still squirm at the mention of power; yet most women are drawn to the concept. As Dr. Marotta field-tested the concepts for her first book, *Power and Wisdom: The New*

Path for Women, the response to invitations for selected South Florida professional women to join a Women of Wisdom Power Breakfast Group was 100 percent acceptance. In order to have the group be an intense, power generating, brainstorming collective versus a networking collective, the group was closed to new members after it was formed, and remained limited in size. Once the word was out about the group, multiple requests were made to join. Clearly, women of achievement are aware of their needs for power training. Yet, out of this achieving group of attorneys, doctors, and businesswomen, one asked, "Can we take the word power out of the title?"

This woman, who has many power behaviors, avoided the term power. Despite a strong maternal role model, she has ambivalent feelings about power. In her viewpoint, power is an uncomfortable word. She views power as something that is forceful and abrasive. Nonetheless, her behaviors in the group demonstrate that despite her discomfort with the word, she uses power effectively. She is comfortable with expressing her opinions and different perspectives. She projects self-confidence and maintains appropriate self-care behaviors with exercise and health. She is an attractive and thoughtful woman who has multiple accomplishments. Yet with all of her demonstrations of power use, she does not want to be viewed as powerful. She believes the myth that power usage involves a lack of consideration for others; when in actuality, power and consideration go hand in hand. The sad reality is that ill-used power in the hands of some has given power "a bad name." Today, women leaders still find women not using the adjective "powerful" to describe themselves.

The dilemma of the negative connotations of power creates a double bind for many women. Even though women may yield power effectively, they are not comfortable with power. This creates an internal conflict, which can limit effectiveness. Limitations in life are something to be removed. Thus, you cannot just engage in powerful behavior, you must have internal comfort with the use of power.

Comfort with power begins with understanding the power you use daily. When you establish goals for your family, for yourself, or for your business, you are exercising power. Managing daily activities, activating decision-making, developing plans — all are exercises of power. When you conduct discussions with an employee or a colleague and brainstorm more effective ways of approaching a problem, you are being powerful. When men and women are in loving relationships with mutual reciprocity, they are expressing their personal power to each other. Power is integral to every moment of every day, and is to be treasured, not avoided. **Power enhances femininity as a nurturing force creating internal strength and calm, and propels you toward effective living.**

Stigma of Power

Power, unfortunately, has taken on negative connotations far afield from its real meaning. A powerful person is seen as someone who dominates or controls others with inappropriate use of force. A powerful person is viewed as one who may be controlling or manipulative, enslaves others, or is a user of people for selfish means. Power has been viewed in a hierarchical way of power *over* others, rather than a power *with* others. The dominant controlling version of power is *power over*. This is the negative end of the continuum. The positive point of the continuum is *power with*. Power with promotes the well-being of self and others, and is inspirational and considerate of others.

Negative Power	Positive Power
Domination = **Power *over***	Inspiration = **Power *within***

Controlling behaviors have the goal of dominating others and generating negativity and adding stress to others. When power is used as power over, it creates oppressiveness and victimizes other people. Controlling behaviors increase suffering and worry and create fear. Controlling behaviors are the hallmark of insecure individuals who need to dominate others for their own self-aggrandizement.

The stigma of power arises from the confusion of power and control. *Webster's* defines control as "to exercise restraint or direction over; dominate; command; to hold and check; curb." Control is the word that embodies dominating others. Control and power can often be confused in your mind. **Power is effectiveness, confidence, and the ability to achieve; it is not control.**

You must recognize that control is a separate word and concept. Unlinking the concept of control from the concept of power is essential for women. Power and control are separate words, separate concepts, and separate constellations of human behavior. Women's ability to incorporate power behaviors will be fast-forwarded when they remove the concept of control from the concept of power. Women need to engage in out-of-the-box thinking and reframe power as effectiveness. Lynn R. Offerman, Ph.D., developer of the Power Apprehension Scale, found that negative attitudes toward power impact the types of influence strategies you use. If you view power negatively, you are at a high risk of limiting your ability to resolve problems. **The term "Positive Power" will be used to facilitate the new cognitive framework of power independent from control.**

Incorrect	Correct
> Uses force	> Creates a peaceful vision
> Results in control of others	> Enhances self-control
> Produces oppression	> Embraces liberation
> Adds stress	> Manages stress
> Causes worry	> Eliminates worry
> Generates negativity	> Generates positivity
> Stifles creativity	> Sparks creativity
> Creates fear	> Limits fear
> Limits personal growth	> Fosters personal growth

Positive Power as a Skill

A person develops Positive Power by learning a range of life strategies. Positive Power is not a genetic component, nor is it an elusive gem that you have to be lucky to unearth. Positive Power is a skill to develop and expand throughout your life. Women need to engage in a new mindset to be able to acquire the skill with greater ease. The new mindset is transformational thinking. Thus, redefining power allows you to activate power. The term "Positive Power" is used to remove the negative perceptions of power.

The key to developing Positive Power skills is to focus on the pronoun *I*. Recognizing that *I* can only control self reveals that *I* is the power trigger to move forward. As you focus on the *I* in your life, it is essential to recognize your strengths and to celebrate those strengths with an inner calm that generates a special charisma. Focusing on your *I* allows you to assume a personal responsibility that is a catalyst to activating initiatives. The *I* focus is the ability to be proactive in your life. The assumption of personal responsibility and the ability to create direction in your life are essential ingredients. You are still considerate and thoughtful to others. You remain a nurturing woman who refuses to be emotionally hooked by your environment. You avoid emotional hooks by using Positive Power tools.

Positive Power as a Life Necessity

Think for a moment. If you are not powerful, you are powerless. Like being in a boat without a rudder, powerlessness tosses you to and fro in the ocean of life. Unable to create a clear direction in your life, you ride the waves of daily living in an unfocused manner, ricocheting through life. Without the focus of Positive Power, your ability to be effective is at the whim of other individuals. You are a woman not in control; you are an ineffective human being.

Powerful behaviors generate positive perceptions, emotions, thoughts, words, attitudes, and proactive actions. Empowered women possess multiple strategies, decreased depression, and reduced anxiety. At the same time, interpersonal skills improve as you become more empowered, more comfortable, and more adept at working with others. As you grow in Positive Power, you become an effective member of family and work teams, and your feeling of well-being allows you to be empathetic and compassionate to others. Also, as a powerful person, you generate a charisma and positive aura that attracts others. As you develop your Positive Power skills, you notice the effects quickly. As Positive Power skills become more and more integrated into your behaviors, you feel calmer and more centered, maximizing your well-being. Positive Power is essential to effective living, essential to your physical and mental well-being, and essential to your quality of life. A life without Positive Power is a life unlived. The message to women is, "power up."

Positive Power and the Glass Ceiling

The acquisition of Positive Power skills is essential to moving beyond the Glass Ceiling, a term first coined in a *Wall Street Journal* article on March 24, 1986. It was used to represent the artificial barrier that prevents qualified women and minorities from advancing to top-level management positions. This phrase captures a wide range of behaviors into a succinct and descriptive term. The Glass Ceiling, like any artificial barrier, robs the organization of the talent of all employees. Whether the organization is government, education, business, or nonprofit, limiting the talents of the staff negatively impacts productivity and stops the organization from realizing its full potential.

The Glass Ceiling Commission was established on November 21, 1991, as part of the Civil Rights Act of 1991. The Department of Labor recognized the need to eliminate barriers to the advancement of women and minorities. The vision of the Glass Ceiling Commission was to foster an enlightenment of national corporate leadership to recognize management diversity is essential for long-term success of the United States in the domestic and global market. Four years later, the formal recommendations of the Glass Ceiling Commission were released. The report, *A Solid Investment: Making Full Use of the National Human Capital*, aptly reflects the Commission's findings that companies that promoted women and minority workers had a higher growth rate. Capitalizing on the talents of all employees translates into a positive impact to the "bottom line."

Moving beyond the Glass Ceiling requires an activation of Positive Power tools. Once you activate your Positive Power tools, you are able to advocate the acceptance of diverse viewpoints and opinions, and incorporate these diverse insights into policy.

Since Dr. Marotta's first book *Power and Wisdom: The New Path for Women* was published in 1999, the new millennium has begun to see women leverage to positions of power. The following is a partial list of such inspirational women.

Forbes lists former U.S. Secretary of State Hilary Clinton as the second most powerful woman in politics in the world (No. 1 is German Chancellor Angela Merkel), and the most powerful woman in U.S. politics. As the former world ambassador of the largest economy on earth, Clinton's advancement of U.S. policy interests focused on women's rights and education development.

Janet Napolitano, former Secretary Department of Homeland Security, oversaw the third largest department with a budget of $48 billion, a staff of 240,000, and twenty-two agencies including FEMA, U.S. Customs and Border Protection, U.S. Citizenship and Immigration Services, the U.S. Coast Guard, the Secret Service, and cyber security.

The 113th Congress of 2013 tops the history books with more women than ever holding seats in the House of Representatives and the Senate. Both legislative bodies have set record high numbers for female representation: seventy-eight in the House and twenty in the Senate. The 2012 election proved the power of the women's vote, and not only returned female incumbents but also brought a record number of female newcomers to Congress, making it the largest class of female newcomers since 1992.

There are now twenty female CEOs (4 percent) running America's largest companies. It is frustrating that that number is actually a record and that more than half obtained the top job between 2011-2012. IBM celebrated its 100-year track record by appointing a woman, Ginni Rometty, to lead the company in 2012. Wal-Mart appointed Rosalind Brewer as its first woman and first African-American to head a subsidiary company, Sam's Club.

What's exciting is that the *mosts* and *firsts* are coming fast and furious. We encourage you to begin lining up for leadership positions by maximizing your strategies for advancement.

Hats off to a few of the many powerful women today:

- Heather Bresch, CEO, Mylan
- Ursula Burns, CEO, Xerox
- Deborah Hersman, Chair, U.S. National Transportation Safety Board
- Garcia Martore, CEO, Gannett
- Denise Morrison, CEO, Campbell Soup
- Deanna Mulligan, CEO, Guardian Life
- Indra Nooyi, CEO, PepsiCo
- Debra Reed, CEO, Sempra Energy
- Irene Rosenfeld, CEO, Modelez International
- Sheryl Sandberg, author, COO, Facebook
- Meg Whitman, CEO, Hewlett-Packard
- Janet Yellen, U.S. Federal Reserve Chair

We began this chapter with a quote from Oprah Winfrey, and we'd like to end it by celebrating her powerful contributions to society: Founder of Harpo Productions, the Oprah Winfrey Network, and the Oprah Winfrey Leadership Academy for Girls. The world's only African-American billionaire, she also has proven to be one of the world's most talented businesswomen, activist for the advancement of women and philanthropist. How will you contribute to the momentum of women in leadership roles?

3

Power Robbers: Be Aware

*"If (women) understood and exercised their power,
they could remake the world."*

— Emily Taft-Douglas, Congresswoman

How Power Robbers Develop

Power robbers are the subtle socialization messages that women receive as they grow up. None of these subtle messages can be totally eliminated from your life. However, as you review the top ten power robbers, you will find that each also has a message to counter these thoughts. Using counter thoughts is a behavioral procedure that is part of a cognitive restructuring clinical intervention. Cognitive restructuring considers how the framework — the outlook that we possess —impacts our behaviors and emotions. The psychological principle is: beliefs generate thoughts; thoughts generate emotions; emotions impact our behavior. A helpful image is to think of a cognitive framework as the frame of a picture. The frame dramatically impacts the visual appeal of the picture. Many times a different frame and matting will change the artistic appeal of the picture. In this same way, our ability to change our framework with different thoughts will generate different emotions and behaviors.

Internal messages, or self-talk, form our belief system, and are absorbed throughout our life. These messages are transmitted through family, friends, and peers. Often, the messages are not communicated directly through speech. The messages are frequently communicated by a subtle reward system. For example, you may never be told directly to be quiet and keep a low profile in a group. However, every time you take the initiative and speak up at the dinner table, your parents and brother give you disapproving looks. Thus, the subtle message is "be quiet." On the other hand, every time your brother speaks up, he is rewarded with encouragement and approving glances. It becomes evident by the differential response to your behaviors that different expectations exist for women and men. These subtle socialization messages are power robbers for women.

Societal messages of different expectations for women and men combine to create stereotypic expectations by gender. The American Psychological Association published a report in the *APA Monitor* that discusses the impact of gender stereotypes. This report profiled the workplace in an article titled *Stereotypes Still Stymie Female Managers,* and discussed multiple research studies that continue to report that female and male leaders receive differential responses. This article and others clearly indicate that gender is an important factor in others' perceptions of appropriate behavior in personal and professional settings.

It is time for women to learn to monitor the power-robbing messages they have been given. As we examine the power robbers in life for women, carefully ask yourself each question. At the close of each power robber, circle the counter thoughts most relevant to you. We encourage you to copy each counter thought and repeat at least once a week. Speaking the counter thought out loud helps you to encode it from your short-term memory to your long-term memory.

Another way to look at this is to view your brain as a computer. You want to counter the "viruses" (the power robbers) in your brain and upload updated software programs (the power lessons). Let's start the process!

POWER ROBBER #1
If I am accommodating and pleasing, I will have many friends and a rewarding life.

Messages From Society

- Can you remember being told to be a good girl and a nice girl?
- Be agreeable and everyone will like you.
- You need to have friends.
- How popular you are is very important.

Questions to Ask Yourself

- Are you very concerned the majority of people like you?
- Are you concerned with others' opinions?
- Is it very important to you that you not disappoint others?
- Do you feel guilty when you disappoint someone?

Kim's Story

Kim is a driven and articulate college graduate, who participated in a competitive university program during Florida's Legislative Session. Her passion for progressive environmental policies paired with a desire to enter the political arena, drove Kim to pursue an internship with an environmental advocacy group in Tallahassee, Florida. During the first two weeks of her internship, the environmental advocacy organization allowed Kim to sit in on meetings with representatives, attend committee meetings, network with Florida's power-house environmental activists and lead an Everglades awareness campaign targeting Florida's universities. Sound like the dream internship? Well yes, in the beginning, her internship created a professional environment that challenged Kim and gave her hope for a potential career in environmental lobbying.

However, as the Florida Session developed, her experience soon changed. Her internship responsibilities transitioned into secretarial and administrative, sitting behind a desk all day booking meetings for her group's lobbyists. She soon lost the "hands-on experience" that every recent college graduate needs for professional success. Suddenly, her internship lacked balance, and her time spent in Tallahassee was not reaching its full potential. Kim faced an ethical and professional dilemma.

While Kim struggled with the idea of leaving her current internship, a position opened up in a House of Representative's office directly working with the Legislative Aide. This position mirrored her political views and the district was close to her hometown. She knew that her role within the House office would maximize her skills and expand her networking opportunities in Tallahassee politics. Kim struggled with people-pleasing behavior versus accepting a strategic professional opportunity. Should she stay in her current position because it would be the "nice" thing to do? She worried about the potential negative consequences of leaving her position with the environmental group. Would her transition blacklist her from potential jobs in the environmental arena? Would this transition question Kim's professional loyalty and commitment in politics?

Kim sought the advice of her peers, professional mentors and the program director. She feared her decision would create unintended professional consequences and this created severe restlessness and anxiety. Analyzing her options, she decided that the professional opportunities of a House internship outweighed pleasing others. Kim started using Positive Power decision-making in her professional career, a skill that will allow her to reach professional success in any field she chooses one day. However, it was not without a significant internal struggle and overcoming her fears.

Negating this power-robbing behavior proved successful for Kim. She became an irreplaceable staffer for her House Representative, directly supporting her Legislative Aide and heading up many of her own projects in the office. This intimate work environment also proved to be beneficial, not only receiving direct mentorships from her Representative, she found other Representatives and staffers in close offices engaged with her, expanding Kim's overall professional experience working in the Florida House of Representatives.

Kim's Positive Power decisions leveraged her career for immeasurable success. Kim's unrelenting commitment to herself and ability to risk displeasing others served her well.

Overview

The recognition that women need to shed people-pleasing behaviors has been encouraged in numerous texts and by influential women. Sheryl Sandberg, chief operating officer of Facebook, listed as *Fortune's* 50 Most Powerful Women in Business and *Time's* 100 Most Influential People in the World, admits in her popular book, *Lean In,* that her desire to be liked by everyone would hold her back professionally and limit her progress. Additionally, she noted her insecurities with the word "power" and its relationship to pleasing others.

Endless pleasing of others robs you of your power. The difficulty of managing this behavior even challenges the most powerful women in America's political and business worlds. Women always will be praised for pleasing others. We also get reinforcement from others by not disappointing them. However, a source of power lies in the ability to give yourself the same kind of care that you would give others.

People-pleasing thoughts often lead to indecisiveness, because what we're *really* doing is relying on the opinions of others to determine our actions. The cornerstone of this behavior is the belief that if you can get others to be pleased with you and approve of you, then you will feel better inside. Actually, the opposite happens when you try to please everybody. You begin to lose your self-respect and become resentful of the people you are trying to please. You do not want to be viewed merely as a hardworking worker bee, or a rubberstamp worker, without the ability to achieve higher positions. Sometimes you need to make tough decisions that will not please people — that can, in fact, upset people. Your growth and opportunities will be limited, without the willingness to make hardline decisions that may displease others.

Counter Thoughts

- Someone being disappointed in me is not a life or death matter.
- Making decisions in the professional arena should be weighed in professional not personal terms.
- My happiness comes from within. I do not depend on approval from the outside world to make me happy.
- I am committed to a program of self-approval and self-affirmation on a daily basis.
- Others' opinions do not define me. If they do not like me or if they reject me, this does not diminish me in any way; this is only their opinion.

- Being liked and approved by others is favorable, but not necessary for professional and personal success.
- I can make choices that nurture me to reach my potential.

POWER ROBBER #2
I want to do it right and not make mistakes.

Messages From Society

- It is more important to get it right rather than finish it.
- You don't want to be embarrassed by making a mistake.
- Mistakes are to be avoided at all costs; take all the time you need to do it right.

Questions to Ask Yourself

- Do you believe all your work must be done preferably better than other people do it?
- Do you scold and criticize yourself when you make mistakes?
- Do you feel you have to work twice as hard as "truly successful people" in order to succeed?
- Do you believe that one mistake ruins everything?
- Do you agonize over mistakes that you make and try to make amends for what you have done?

April's Story

Lack of power can be expressed in many ways. April is an example of a woman rendered ineffective by a fear of making mistakes. Fear of being wrong can cause a power drain leading to powerlessness. April entered my office in tears. She was in her early forties, married with two teenage children. April was a college graduate who was experiencing extreme job stress, moving through six jobs in five years. She reported disrupted sleep, depressed mood, and feeling overwhelmed. She stated, "I have trouble making decisions. I am afraid of being wrong." Her fear of making mistakes caused her to have job paralysis, which repeatedly led to dismissal.

Each time April had a decision to make, she would ask everyone in the office for his or her input. She would make list after list of pros and cons. Although she was highly competent, April was paralyzed by her fears. She missed deadlines and frustrated upper management. April began to be viewed as a roadblock to progress.

April's latest manager completed her performance review and placed her on probation. In therapy, we shifted the focus to learning how to conduct a cost-benefit analysis. April began to develop a new cognitive template: Every decision has limitations. As she progressed, she began to make decisions more quickly. She became less and less concerned about being "right" and more committed to getting the job done to the best of her ability. She became more realistic in her expectations for herself.

During treatment sessions, April was able to reframe mistakes as an opportunity for learning. Additionally, she was able to focus on the value of taking initiative; and mistakes were normalized as part of the learning curve of a new job. April's ability to develop risk-taking skills and decrease her fears of making mistakes resulted in increased initiative and job stability.

The outcome: April's manager removed her from probation. For the first time in five years, she was confident this was a job she was going to be able to keep.

Overview

Do you remember being told to be careful? Make sure you do it right! Don't make any mistakes! That is the beginning of the power-robbing message of perfection, the installation of the fear of making mistakes. The desire always to do it right and not make mistakes often leads to the trap of perfectionism. Perfectionist individuals are extremely critical, and have a high level of dissatisfaction. Your drive for perfection causes you to set up unrealistic expectations, which can lead to a failure cycle. In life, perfection does not exist. You need to readjust your thinking to the concept of adequate behaviors.

Avoidance of mistakes is unrealistic. Mistakes are part and parcel of a learning process. Mistake avoidance is a drive for perfection. Often a deep-seated fear of failure and rejection is underneath the drive for perfection. This fear causes you to be your own critic. When failure ultimately occurs due to unrealistic expectations, perfectionists rebuke themselves and withdraw. This fear of failure can be a businessperson's biggest stumbling block. Being fearful leads to staying with safe behaviors and not "pushing the envelope."

Leadership requires moving beyond safe behaviors with creative initiative. You need to push the envelope to create a higher probability of success. If you always stay in a safe zone to avoid mistakes, your success will be limited. You need to expend effort with a willingness to absorb mistakes. The hidden danger of perfectionism and fearfulness of mistakes is that you become so focused on "doing it right" that you often are oblivious to the political atmosphere. In the majority of cases, multiple right ways of doing something exist. You can go down multiple paths to reach the same outcome. A fearfulness of mistakes causes a rigidity, which limits openness to achieving business goals in another manner. As part of a management team, a woman's openness to other options is crucial.

Perfectionism can be a trap that saps our energy and bogs down our career path. Although work must be well done, each work sample does not have to be a masterpiece. Performance standards must be viewed from a cost-benefit analysis of value received for the effort taken. All tasks can be done over and over, but at some point, enough is enough.

Quality work can be completed in time-efficient means. Productivity and an ability to move to the next task are essential. A large element of perfectionism is avoiding criticism. However, if you avoid all criticism, you become paralyzed.

Mistakes are integral to moving forward efficiently. People make missteps from the beginning of their lives to the end — whether it's the imperfect faltering movements of a toddler or an oversight as a manager. Learn to tolerate criticism, accept errors, be open to different approaches, and move toward your goals. Forward movement supersedes a concern with mistakes. Criticism avoiders focus on anticipating the reactions of others versus productivity and meeting goals. No matter how excellent your work product, you cannot protect yourself from all criticism. Criticism is not a career-stopper; however, not meeting your goals certainly limits your opportunities.

Counter Thoughts

- Perfection is an unrealistic expectation.
- Avoiding failure is paralyzing.
- I want to be conscientious, not perfect.
- I can only make the best decision at the time.
- I can be myself; I do not have to prove myself.
- I see my mistakes as temporary setbacks and learning opportunities.

POWER ROBBER #3
I want to avoid upsetting others.

Messages From Society

- Put your best face forward; don't let anyone know you are upset.
- If you can't say anything nice, keep quiet.
- You get more with honey than vinegar.

Questions to Ask Yourself

- Do you find yourself worrying about others' possible negative reactions?

- When conflict begins to arise, do you find yourself engaging in soothing behaviors?
- Are you unable to communicate your own frustrations or upset feelings directly?

Angela's Story

Emotional hooks are important to avoid, as the clinical case of Angela demonstrates. Angela is an attractive, 32-year-old, married, retail executive with one preschool-age child. She was referred to therapy by her primary physician because of panic attacks she experienced from a fear of driving. When she experienced one of these attacks, her heart beat rapidly, a lump rose in her throat, her hands perspired, and she felt a constriction in her chest.

Angela was a community leader, involved with several charitable organizations. As therapy progressed, it became evident that Angela wanted to avoid upsetting others. She had difficulty setting limits with her staff, her colleagues, her friends, and her family. She would respond to requests with an affirmative answer without any consideration of other demands on her time. Angela was a classic case of a panic attack patient whose body was reacting to her overdoing behaviors.

During therapy, Angela learned a range of limit-setting skills starting with not responding to requests immediately. She also learned to evaluate all requests carefully. A discussion in therapy uncovered an issue with her administrative staff. Angela stated how she appreciated her administrative staff staying late to help her with work. On further discussion, a review of job responsibilities revealed that her assistant was not tending to her tasks during the workday. Angela was, in fact, staying after hours to help her assistant complete her tasks. In her desire not to upset anyone, she overlooked the reality of her assistant's poor job performance.

Once she stepped back from the situation and realized that she was emotionally hooked by her assistant's inefficiency, a chain of events ensued. Angela reviewed the administrative assistant's job description, held a performance review with her and discovered that the assistant was spending excessive office time on personal phone calls rather than work. Angela's panic attacks began to decrease dramatically as her administrative assistant appropriately assumed responsibility for her own work. Once Angela was able to understand and identify her *I* needs clearly and not be hooked by the fear of upsetting others, her panic attacks gradually ceased.

Overview

The underlying premise of the message to not upset others is based on an irrational belief. The irrational belief is that you can control someone else's feelings with your behaviors. We do not have the power to create or dictate feelings in others. Individuals are responsible for their beliefs and thought patterns, which in turn creates their feelings. Thus, it is impossible to predict what behaviors will upset others. You can act in a charming manner and still upset someone.

Not only are you unable to control another's reaction to you, but life necessitates a certain degree of conflict. Going out of your way to avoid conflict also avoids constructive confrontation, prevents decision-making, and creates an indecisive persona. If you always attempt to avoid upsetting others, you become a social chameleon. Conflict is an inevitable part of life and you need to develop appropriate conflict-resolution skills. Avoiding conflict robs you of the ability to develop these skills. The danger of being a social chameleon is that you are so agreeable that you become a "yes" person. As a "yes" person, you reduce your authority and credibility.

Women have long received a strong societal message to not "ruffle any feathers." Women are continually cast into the role of peacemaker. Not only is the avoidance of upsetting others and conflict unrealistic, such avoidance also predisposes women to constantly apologize to avoid negative feelings. The pattern of always saying, "I'm sorry," creates an image of powerlessness and engenders condescending behaviors. These images and reactions do not help women position themselves as potential leaders.

The flip side of not upsetting anyone means that you cannot express any feelings of being upset yourself or discuss any angry feelings. Women are coached not to express negative feelings, because it will damage relationships. Women are encouraged to remain calm. This suppression of anger produces high frustration, feelings of weakness, lower self-esteem, and limits effectiveness. When you hold back your reactions, you are not interacting with others realistically. You are placing yourself in danger of being mistreated, because you are not alerting others to their problem behaviors. You need to respect yourself and request respect from others to be effective, productive, and recognized for your leadership skills.

Counter Thoughts

- I am not responsible for the feelings of others.
- Someone liking me is not as important as me liking myself.
- There is more than one way of looking at things, and I am entitled to my opinion.
- I have the right to express annoyances and do not have to escalate into anger.
- I can engage in constructive negotiation and not damage my relationships.
- I need to give feedback on problem behaviors so adjustments can be made.

POWER ROBBER #4
If there is a problem, it is my fault.

Messages From Society

- Remember you are the one who is responsible.
- You are the caretaker for others.
- Being responsible is very important.
- You need to watch out for others.

Questions to Ask Yourself

- Do you find yourself asking: Oh, my goodness, what did I do?
- Do you question yourself regularly?
- Do you spend a lot of time engaging in worry activities?
- Do problems make you uncomfortable?

Sheila's Story

Sheila is a 37-year-old entrepreneur. She is a creative woman who developed a highly successful new phone application. An executive client, who was concerned that Sheila was slipping into a depression, referred her to Dr. Marotta. On meeting Sheila, her eyes darted around the room, she hung her head forward, and it was difficult to obtain eye contact. Her agitation was evident, because her hands were trembling. Sheila began the session by saying how sorry she was that she was five minutes late, how terrible a day she was having due to yelling at an employee, and to pardon her appearance because she got caught in a rainstorm and her clothes were wrinkled. She worried about sitting on the couch and leaving a water stain. She forgot her checkbook and apologized for her oversight at least six times. The checkbook apologies continued despite the fact that our office accepts credit cards, and payment was not an issue. Clearly, Sheila was a master of negative self-talk.

Not only was Sheila engaging in negative statements, her internal self-critic was even more extreme. As the sessions progressed, I asked Sheila to tally the number of negative statements she made each hour. After one week of daily tallies, Sheila was averaging forty-two negative statements every thirty minutes. A large percentage of her statements were self-berating for others' activities and were not directly related to her own behavior.

The gathering of her negative self-talk data was an eye opener for Sheila. To assist her in limiting negative self-talk, I suggested a simple thought-stopping intervention: put a rubber band around her wrist and snap it every time she caught herself in either an internal or external negative self-statement. The first week she began using this technique, she had to wear sweaters so she would not have welts on her arms. Since my clinical practice is located in South Florida, she told her staff she was testing a new deodorant and needed to wear sweaters to make sure she was sweating appropriately. I am not sure whether her employees believed her deodorant-testing story; however, Sheila made significant progress in reducing her negative self-talk. She appropriately limited her perceptions of responsibility and increased her positive self-talk.

Two years later, Sheila called for a coaching session. When she arrived in my office, the difference in her appearance and demeanor was startling. She maintained excellent eye contact, confidently entered the room, and possessed engaging charisma.

Overview

Women are conditioned to accept responsibility for everything. There are several jokes about problems in life being due to ineffective mothering. Mother and mother-in-law jokes proliferate. Women, with their biological template of nurturing, are vulnerable to being over-responsible. This over-responsibility causes them to assume blame for situations over which, in reality, they have no control.

Women's predisposition to worry and guilt feelings causes them to blame themselves for problems. When problems arise, women become uncomfortable and engage in immediate worry that in some way they may have caused the problem. Worry can be a destructive emotion, and guilty feelings compound worry. Even physical impairment can result from excessive concerns and guilt. Worry is often referred to as a malfunction of the mind that can increase physical disease. Worrying is helpful only as a first reaction to identify a problem. Incessant worry taxes the mind, and the "worry loop" becomes so consuming that you lose your power to engage in adequate problem solving.

Expressing concern and engaging in problem solving is productive. The key to effective and productive behavior is to accept appropriate responsibility. Other people also have responsibilities, and you are not fully responsible for everything. You can make your contributions. You cannot control the total outcome. Worry and guilt are limiting behaviors. You want to be responsible, but within limits. You can control worry and guilt by recognizing the limits of what you are able to accomplish. The only value in worrying is to identify a problem. If you have impact on the presenting problem, it is important to move from worry to problem solving. If you have no impact on the issue, it is best to redirect your energies.

Controlling the use of apologies is also an issue in loss of power. Women, with their nurturing behaviors, often express concern with "I am sorry." Expressions of concern must be expressed carefully. Your concern may be perceived as either "rubbing it in," or interpreted as though you contributed to the problem. Unfortunately, saying "I am sorry" can be misinterpreted as placing yourself in a one-down position of fault that robs you of your power. Avoid apologies, and express concern without the use of the *I* pronoun. You need to step back and be a responsible individual, but not the over-responsible one.

Counter Thoughts

- Problems are a natural part of living.
- I do the best I can; I need to monitor my guilt.
- I cannot change the past, I can only move on.
- I am responsible for my own behaviors.
- I cannot control the full outcome.
- Worry is nonproductive.

POWER ROBBER #5

I need to be polite and not make direct requests.

Messages From Society

- Remember, it is bad manners to ask for anything.
- Wait for people to ask you; it is rude to make requests.

- Be polite, be a nice girl and don't make demands.
- Be considerate and you will be rewarded.

Questions to Ask Yourself

- Do you preface your requests with a permission-giving phrase such as, may I, can I, do you think?
- Do you approach a request in a deferential manner?
- Do you ask for permission before you ask a question?
- Do you take the time to organize your requests?
- Do you avoid making requests?

Anna's Story

Anna is an intelligent, creative undergraduate pursuing a degree in Engineering. As the first person in her family to pursue a bachelor's degree, her parents believe her high grades in math and science necessitated that Anna pursue a career in engineering.

Although Anna exhibited a unique ability and interest in digital media, her polite and non-confrontational personality resulted in her engaging in parent-pleasing behavior. She sought the approval from her family and began an education in engineering — a major she lacked interest in. Semesters went by and Anna saw minimal academic success in her classes. The precision-oriented and cut-throat competiveness of engineering classes created Anna's apathetic commitment to her major. She became discouraged and unhappy with her classes and professors.

For the first time in her life, Anna experienced academic failure — an experience she found debilitating. Anna was unable to maximize her undergraduate experience, stuck in a profession she severely disliked to make her parents proud. Many semesters went by and Anna held on to her major, seeking approval from her parents and avoiding direct requests of what she wanted from her education and, ultimately, her professional career. After this draining experience, Anna recognized that it was important for her to lead a life of her own and changed her major to reflect her interests. Although she had a passion for education and the arts, her years of politeness and accommodating behaviors hampered her early years in college.

Anna went home and spoke with her parents and explained she lacked passion for engineering and wished to change her major to graphic design. There was a heated argument, because her change in major would extend her education for an additional year. When she went to bed that night, she could hear her parents arguing. It was a tense few days in the household. After Sunday dinner, the family spoke again. Her parents agreed to her change in majors but stated that she would have to take out loans for the additional year. Anna was willing to accept the responsibility of her choices. Today, her change in majors has reinvigorated her attitude towards higher education. Presently, she is in her final year of graphic design and has accepted an exciting job opportunity in Los Angeles upon graduation.

Overview

Courtesy to others is an appropriate sign of mutual respect. However, overly deferential politeness and indirectness undermines your ability to reach your goals. Being excessively polite and indirect creates an image of passivity and a lack of strength. Direct requests improve the clarity of communication.

Women are subtly socialized to be indirect. Women need to learn to engage in more powerful dialogues. For example, "I don't have enough time to finish the project," would be better stated: "The tentative schedule does not allow for completion of the project" or "Let's have a meeting and reassess the priority schedule for the project." A more direct communication pattern focuses on the issue and controls the female tendency for indirectness. In the following examples, the direct communication pattern also keeps the focus on the issues and not on personal performance.

Women are encouraged to be deferential, which creates a behavior pattern of asking permission, waiting for the right moment to initiate a request, and waiting for opportunities, rather than creating opportunities. By waiting for others to take the initiative, you avoid the risk of rejection or disagreement. However, you also limit your opportunities. You become constricted and limit your communication effectiveness. You hold back and waste time.

As evidenced in the socialization pattern of power robbers, a consistent theme exists for women to stay "safe" and not do anything that would be misconstrued or offensive to anyone. This places women in a double bind of preventing them from creating a direct path to their goal. Not only are your goals made more difficult to reach, you engage in "double-speak" versus clarity. Examples of this problematic "double-speak" and the hidden message of asking permission are the following:

Example 1:

Indirect request: "Could you please double-check your email? I did not get a reply to the email I sent you last week."
Direct request: "Here is a hard copy of the high-priority email. Let's take a few minutes to review it together; a decision has to be made."

Example 2:

Indirect request: "I found a very interesting convention that might be helpful in planning for my new management team. Would you mind, within the next week, sitting down and evaluating it with me?"
Direct request: "Here is a superb conference that dovetails exactly with the new management project you assigned me. I recommend that it immediately be included in my convention plans for the year."

The ability to make direct requests is essential to goal achievement. These requests must be stated in the most powerful manner, which avoids any image of asking permission. Women, with their programming for indirectness, have a tendency to talk around the issues rather than get to the bottom line. The more directness you possess, the more clarity you will have in your communications. You will increase the probability of receiving your requests and be able to reach your goals with more ease.

Counter Thoughts

- I can be courteous without being deferentially polite.
- Making requests does not require asking permission.
- Indirectness slows the progress of my goals.
- Direct requests are necessary for effective communication.
- Clarity in communication brings you closer to your goals.

4

Positive Power

Lessons: Learn New Skills

"...women are certainly not invisible, any longer, nor are they any longer represented merely as victims."

— Sandra Bern, Author, Researcher

Why Power Skills Are Necessary

Women have surged into the workplace in record numbers, and now working women are the norm, rather than the exception. This shift in women's roles may result in confrontational situations for which you have never been trained. As you reviewed in the previous chapter, subtle socialization messages may undermine personal effectiveness and make it difficult for you to reach your goals. What would be the outcome if society gave you different lessons? What would happen if you were encouraged to develop a different belief system?

In chapter 3, counter thoughts were used to stop power drains. In chapter 4, affirmations are used to introduce new lessons in Positive Power. Each of the following lessons is keyed to help you reduce the power drain of the power robber. As an example, Power Robber #1 deals with accommodating and people-pleasing behaviors, and Lesson #1 teaches you the more effective messages of limit setting and engaging in self-care. This chapter provides opportunities to begin developing new Positive Power skills. Once you become aware of the subtle power robbers, you'll find the lessons in this chapter allow you to begin imagining yourself as a powerful individual. In the words of Gloria Steinem quoted in Helene Robbins-Lerner's book *Our Power as Women*: "In order to expand our power as women, first we need to imagine our power. The imagination of change is the first step toward change."

Positive Power lessons clearly are not suggestions for women to mimic men. A major theme of this book is realizing the ineffectiveness and limiting nature of mimicking men or holding males up as the ideal, which is referred to as androcentrism. The lessons in this chapter teach women to activate Positive Power and increase effectiveness.

As we discussed in earlier chapters, women too often focus on the needs of others and do not factor in their own needs. The purpose of these lessons is to create a balance. Women want to maintain consideration for others; however, they want relationships to be reciprocal. Interaction with others needs to be a two-way street.

The Positive Power lessons identified in this next section discuss in detail each lesson for moving beyond the power robbers. If you answer "yes" to the questions provided, you are already using some of the lessons to gain power. You need to focus on the questions where you answer "no" or where you are uncertain or uncomfortable with your answer. As you learn the Positive Power lessons, affirmations replace the counter thoughts listed in chapter 3. In this chapter, you are taking the next step. In addition to countering power-robbing messages, you begin to "power up" with new messages to activate your Positive Power behaviors. The affirmations are part of your new "software program," and are the cognitive templates to imprint on your mind.

POSITIVE POWER LESSON #1
I need to set limits and engage in adequate self-care.

Questions to Ask Yourself

- Am I at ease saying no to more than I can do?
- Am I careful about volunteering for new tasks?
- Do I consider my needs for rest, health, nutrition, and exercise in my daily schedule?
- Do I give myself time to rejuvenate?

Moving Beyond

Pleasing and accommodating others can easily lead to a life of overextension. The charming woman who always accommodates and pleases others drains herself of power, and often runs out of hours at the end of the day. A powerful woman values her time and recognizes her energy and time limits. As the multitude of life options increases, it is important to recognize your limits. Sally Helgelsen, in her insightful diary studies of powerful women, *The Female Advantage*, noted that the women she followed practiced deliberate pacing tactics to rejuvenate and maintain their energy and productivity.

The problem for women is that culture praises accommodating behaviors. You receive reinforcement for not disappointing others. However, Positive Power lies in the ability to give yourself the same kind of care you give to others. A balance needs to exist among work intensity, exercise, adequate nutrition, socializing, and other needs. The critical balance is achieved when you remember to consider a given request before responding. Oftentimes, you may forget to consider yourself and become "emotionally hooked" by the requesting person. It is essential to remember you have the ability to take time to choose your response. Engaging in actions based on a careful assessment of data and a consideration of your life balance is an important lesson to learn.

Barriers to appropriate limit setting and adequate self-care are the internal "shoulds." Every time you place a "should" on yourself, you need to examine the request. "Shoulds" are internal messages of obligation, rather than thoughtful decisions of productive choices. You do not want to be pulled by a demanding list of "shoulds." Every time you use the internal self-talk of "should," ask yourself: Is this necessary? Is this productive? Is this the best use of my time?

One of the most important ways to deal with the "shoulds" is to translate "shoulds" to "coulds." This translation allows you to recognize that you have an option. You have the option to say "yes" and you have the option to say "no." Recognizing your options is an important part of limit-setting skills.

There may be a tendency to avoid limit setting because you fear conflict. When you make a decision to do something, another activity goes undone. This often will cause conflict with someone who has a different set of priorities; however, conflict is a necessary part of living. As you assess your options, one variable to factor into your evaluation is the resistance you may receive from others.

Conflict is an intricate part of life, not a negative experience. Conflict is also the natural outgrowth of diversity in cultures, opinions, and expectations. A conflict represents an opportunity for constructive communication. Conflict brings out in the open different ways of think-ing and behaving and differences in values and priorities. Conflicts challenge us to manage our lives in ways that use our differences for own mutual growth and benefit.

To weigh all the personal cost and benefit factors, you need to pos-sess a clear understanding of your own priorities and make beneficial decisions. Maintaining productive behaviors means you need to take steps not to push yourself too hard. If you feel burned out, tense, or ir-ritable, then you need to reassess and change your direction. You need to be able to cancel or renegotiate requirements, and not be afraid of disappointing someone else. You need to be your own primary self-care agent. You are responsible for creating a tolerable and manageable life.

Healthy-Selfish

In order to lead a productive, balanced life, you need to learn the behaviors of healthy-selfish. Healthy-selfish behaviors have the com-ponents of limit setting and an attention to adequate self-care. Limits allow us to manage time, and attention to adequate self-care allows us to balance needs. A helpful imagery is to imagine a seesaw. Do you remember when you were a child and the fun you would have going up and down, up and down? Life as a child on a seesaw can be exhilarating. However, if you live your life on a seesaw, you are constantly propelled from high to low in an exhausting scenario. Imagine that same seesaw with the task side balanced by the play side, now you have created equi-librium. This life balance allows appreciation and enjoyment of work and play and a nurturing of self that is essential to both physical and mental health.

It's also important to control your enthusiasm for life. As an individ-ual interested in many activities, you probably want to engage in more activities than there are hours in the day. An enthusiasm for life is a wonderful attribute. However, it has to be balanced by the reality of lim-ited hours. Time is the one commodity you cannot purchase in a store.

Therefore, time is invaluable. You need to protect your time and energy by engaging in personal planning and establishing boundaries on your willingness and enthusiasm.

You do not live a life of simplicity. You lead a life of multiplicity, which can lead to fragmentation rather than unification. Conflicting demands create a whirlwind of activity that can leave you in turmoil. Your mindset is to see yourself as internally centered with clear limits, no matter how chaotic your life may be. A helpful analogy is the eye of a hurricane. Although a lot of maiming debris may be floating around the center, the eye itself is tranquil. Even if your life is like a hurricane, you can maintain your internal center with stabilizing guidelines of clear limits.

A barrier to maintaining consistency with limit setting and self-care is the difficulty of saying no and disappointing others. The strong socialization that women receive to be pleasing and accommodating causes them to feel guilty when they establish limits and engage in healthy-selfish behaviors.

The guilt feelings a woman may experience need to be countered. It is impossible to go through life and engage in healthy-selfish behaviors without feeling some level of guilt. The objective is not to eliminate guilt, but to moderate guilt and maintain the focus on healthy-selfish behaviors. The key dimensions of healthy-selfish behaviors are the ability to set limits in terms of others' requests and demands, maintain adequate time management, and plan adequate self-care, including exercise and nutrition. Healthy-selfish behaviors are the key to discovering and keeping your emotional equilibrium and a centered, calm control of your life. *A powerful woman is a healthy-selfish woman.*

Can you tell where you are on the scale of healthy-selfish behaviors? Do you say the words healthy-selfish and feel comfortable? Is your desk drowning in unread material? Is your voicemail clogged with backup calls? Do you find yourself avoiding phone calls and contact because you have so many incomplete tasks? If this reminds you of some of your behaviors, then recognize that the lesson of healthy-selfish, with limit setting and life-balanced components, is an essential lesson. Guilt may be a block to your healthy-selfish behaviors, and it is a psychological phenomenon that must be controlled and countered. It is helpful to think of your guilt as a thermometer. Imagine a guilt thermometer range of one to ten; you always want to use Positive Power tools to lower your guilt thermometer to below five. Overcoming guilt allows healthy-selfish behaviors to flourish.

Kate's Story

Kate is an involved campus leader at her university. She is entering her senior year in college and has become extensively involved in a variety of student activities. Her willingness to meet and network with university students through club rowing, student government, and an all-women acapella group allowed Kate an opportunity to become involved but left her exhausted and over-extended. Weekdays were spent in class, and weeknights were spent attending meetings and practices. This left little time for creating a consistent schedule for working out, cooking, and studying.

Kate would stay up late at night to keep up with her challenging coursework. Balancing all of her academic responsibilities and social engagements became emotionally and physically exhausting. She worried if she dropped certain organizations she would lose relationships she had spent three years building.

Kate also recognized the added pressure of graduation and her upcoming transition to the "real world" meant additional responsibilities. She examined the time she spent doing extracurricular activities and decided to be healthy-selfish by taking a step back from extracurricular activities to focus on her health, classes, and graduation. She would only be involved in the activities she valued most. And guess what, her friends totally understood.

The extra time allowed Kate to focus on her top priorities. She was succeeding in her classes, cooking healthy meals, engaging in fitness, and focusing on finding a job after graduation. Kate believed she was engaging in adequate self-care by balancing her academic responsibilities and personal goals. Kate's ability to make changes in her life and overcome her fear of losing her friends sparked a conversation among her peers. Her friendship network began to reevaluate their responsibilities and followed Kate's lead. Remember, there always needs to be a leader.

Affirmations

- As I engage in adequate self-care, I maintain my energy for my life's tasks.
- I focus on my own internal gauge of self-care and comfort.
- I listen to my inner voice and balance my life.
- I want to be considerate of others, not consumed by others.
- A disappointment is not a disaster.
- Healthy-selfish behaviors allow me to be considerate of others and myself.
- Living healthy-selfish results in a balanced life.

POSITIVE POWER LESSON #2

I welcome mistakes as an indicator I am pushing my limits and being all I can be.

Questions to Ask Yourself

- Do you avoid double and triple checking your work?
- Are you comfortable with the suggestion you may have made a mistake?
- Are you glad when an error is found so you can work on the solution?
- When you make a mistake, are you able to move forward without engaging in self-critical behaviors?
- Do you take the opportunity to learn from your mistakes?

Moving Beyond

This is a significant shift from the power robber idea of avoiding mistakes and seeking perfectionism. The new cognitive mindset is that mistakes are an integral part of learning. John Dewey, a noted American educator, founded his educational philosophy on the concept of "learning by doing." Learning is an ongoing process, and trial and error are often the best teachers. Difficulties challenge your talents; surmounting them is rewarding. However, with reward comes the risk of making mistakes, which can cause you to freeze in fear. You need to recognize mistakes as profound learning opportunities. Oprah Winfrey stated in her commencement address at Wesleyan University, "There is no such thing as failure. Mistakes happen in your life to bring into focus more clearly who you really are."

You may react fearfully to mistakes, often replaying them over and over in your mind. You also may become defensive and bristle when someone suggests you made an error. These reactions consume time and energy — and are not constructive. When you view mistakes as adding valuable information to your internal data bank, you begin to appreciate their value.

Rather than being devastated by mistakes, reward yourself for stretching and moving into new areas. Mistakes can lead to growth and understanding. Develop a tolerance for mistakes, and you begin to function more independently, with increased confidence. You begin to initiate new actions.

Expand your ability to handle constructive criticism by reframing it. Instead of seeing it as negative, label it as positive feedback, which when integrated into your belief system allows you to increase productivity. Your openness to constructive criticism helps you grow. The more you learn, the more productive and creative you become.

When you are intolerant of mistakes, your response to a critical remark becomes one of personal hurt, which then turns into an emotional disability. The realization that everyone makes mistakes enables you to handle criticism and protects you. Accepting you are not perfect and viewing feedback as constructive is like putting on a suit of armor — it shields you and makes you a more effective individual.

Brittany's Story

Brittany, a 42-year-old married female with a 5-year-old child, was offered a position as a medical office manager. Previously, she was a supervisor at a telemarketing company that sold impact-resistant windows. She was new to the medical arena. However, she had supervised others and mentored her sales team. Her references reflected people management skills as well as organizational skills.

She became familiar with the doctors, staff, and their expectations. Even though she is an intelligent capable woman, Brittany was overwhelmed by the medical lingo and the fast pace of the office. She found herself reacting defensively as requests increased. She felt reproached, pushed, and under a microscope. She started to dread going to work and criticized herself for changing jobs and "upsetting the apple cart." Her sleep was disrupted and her energy low.

A few weeks into her employment, the managing doctor called her into his office. He said what impressed the doctors most throughout the interview process were her marketing, customer relations, and organizational skills. He explained they were aware she was new to the medical field and they expected she would need time to get up to speed. He encouraged her to relax and be realistic about the time it takes to switch from one field to another.

Brittany recognized that it was better to misstep early on. She shifted to a learning mode and decreased her defensiveness. She pushed herself not to worry about being seen as incompetent and turned into a question-asking machine.

One year later, the office expanded and two new doctors were added. Brittany hired an assistant manager to help manage the expanded office and received a bonus.

Affirmations

- I will engage in self-correction, not self-condemnation.
- Corrective input from others is to be welcomed, not defended.
- A mistake is an opportunity to learn.
- If there is a mistake, I will be gentle and tolerant with myself.
- Mistakes are part of my humanity, and I refuse to condemn myself for any shortcomings or mistakes.
- As a seeker of excellence, not a perfectionist, I am open to direction and constructive criticism.

POSITIVE POWER LESSON #3

I seek respect of others and recognize some people will be uncomfortable around me.

Questions to Ask Yourself

- Are you able to tolerate an uncomfortable feeling?
- Are you able to consistently and credibly state your position?
- Do you value being respected more than being popular?
- Can you disagree with someone and not have it contaminate the relationship?
- Can you tolerate being questioned by others without becoming defensive and taking it personally?

Moving Beyond

It is important to become less concerned with other people's reactions and more concerned with maintaining the clarity of your own beliefs, values, and behaviors. Personal credibility and respect become valued more than being an "agreeable woman" who never upsets anyone.

Life is not an ongoing popularity contest; it is a balance of differing needs and responsibilities. You become aware there are many different perspectives and viewpoints. The most important behaviors are credible and respectful of others' opinions. However, being respectful of other perspectives does not mean you have to defer to others. A healthy relationship is able to tolerate constructive disagreement. Psychological research demonstrates that even in romantic relationships, intimacy requires a certain amount of conflict.

Since disagreements and different levels of conflict are inevitable, the ability to stand your ground while respecting others' perspectives is essential. You also need to be able to verbalize your positions and feelings with clarity. Disagreements do not have to be win-lose encounters; they can be negotiated compromises. Often a healthy respect for different viewpoints gives all viewpoints credence in personal or business negotiations. Conflict resolution skills focus on an open exchange of information and the willingness to thoroughly examine all viewpoints to reach agreement or consensus.

Not only must women be able to tolerate and discuss different viewpoints, they need to recognize that even though they are entering the workforce in large numbers, they are still an anomaly in many settings. As a result, gender in and of itself may cause some personal discomfort. Often, interpersonal discomfort opens the door for discussion, and uncomfortable interpersonal interactions can be seen as a challenge to resolve the discomfort and develop a mutually respectful rapport. The lesson is to shift your focus from a concern with others' feelings — over which you have no control — to conducting yourself in a manner that promotes respect.

Jewel's Story

A famous singer had been contracted to sing at the Chicago Opera house. The concert was sold out. The anticipation and excitement were palpable as the house manager took the stage. "Ladies and gentlemen, thank you for coming. I regret to tell you that due to illness, the headliner you've all come to hear will not be performing tonight. However, we have an exciting newcomer to entertain you." The fans groaned so loud, they failed to hear the stand-in's name.

The back-up singer believed this was her time to shine and gave the performance of her life. She refused to be affected by the audience's disappointment and called on her confidence to block the negative energy of the crowd. When she finished, there was an uncomfortable silence. She raised her head and smiled, knowing she had performed her best. As she gazed out over the audience, people rose to their feet with applause.

Her confidence in herself allowed her to seize this opportunity. She refused to be emotionally hooked by the audience's disappointment. What others could have perceived as a disaster, she seized as an opportunity to present a performance to be remembered.

Affirmations

- Being respected by others is more important than being liked.
- Disagreements are a healthy exchange of different viewpoints.
- Constructive conflict can strengthen relationships.
- As a female, I need to be tolerant of male colleagues who are still adjusting to changes in the workforce.
- My goal is to be effective and productive.

POSITIVE POWER LESSON #4

I need to engage in positive self-talk and monitor over-responsibility.

Questions to Ask Yourself

- Do you assess your mistakes to learn from them rather than to criticize yourself?
- Do you rarely berate yourself?

- Do you take time to engage in positive self-talk?
- Do you separate what you are responsible for from others?
- Are you committed to generating positivity in your life?
- Do you spend time in daily positive mindercise?

Moving Beyond

Over-responsibility is a trap that causes you to engage in self-blame and to feel guilty when problems emerge — problems for which you may not have responsibility or solutions. Assuming responsibility is important, but over-assuming responsibility for matters beyond your control can lead to guilt. Guilt and worry fuel negative self-talk. Negative self-talk creates a self-defeating cycle, which undermines effectiveness and the use of Positive Power. Positive self-talk allows you to achieve your goals and generates good feelings. Positive self-talk involves talking to yourself about past successes, how you overcame obstacles and how good it felt. Positive talking also can encompass positive imagining. You want to imagine achieving your goals. Imagining and visioning help program your mind. As you program your mind with positives, you help to manage your mind's productions.

We talk to ourselves continuously. Our brains are perpetually active and our inner statements have the ability to affect us dramatically. In order to unleash your Positive Power, you want to be sure you encourage yourself with self-celebrating thoughts. By creating a constant stream of positive self-talk, you overcome discouraging messages.

Self-talk is not just comprised of random words. Self-talk impacts our ability to perform and creates our emotions. Positive self-talk generates beliefs in you. An easy way to remember is to use the mnemonic: "To Be The First": Thoughts (T) lead to beliefs (B) generating additional thoughts (T), which create feelings (F). It is important to recognize you create the reality of your world by your self-talk.

Since self-talk is so vital to both mental and physical health, you want to engage in daily mindercise. Part of your mindercise is to study the environment, gather information, and challenge your mind. Additional mindercise includes a program of daily mediating or reading an affirmation book to continue to generate a positive, internal, self-talk focus. This proactive self-talk focus is essential to maintaining emotional equilibrium. Positive self-talk also facilitates the release of endorphins in your system, which helps you maintain both physical and psychological health.

Not only is self-talk important, it is also imperative to know that you are only responsible for *your* actions. Further, you do the best you can do at the moment with the information you have. It's important to avoid "second guessing" yourself and criticizing yourself for past behaviors. Remember, when you assess yourself backward, you include new pieces of data, which you did not possess at the time of your decision. The past is important, because we learn from it, but the most important focus is the present. The seventy-percent rule is an effective guideline to building and sustaining Positive Power. Seventy percent of your thoughts and energy needs to be anchored in the present. Twenty percent needs to be anchored in the past, because the past provides a database of learning experiences. Ten percent is reserved for the future, where we set goals. Since goals are constantly reassessed in a rapidly changing environment, you must use your ten percent to keep the goals fresh and in your sights. Still, your greatest energy needs to be focused on the present, since you can readily impact the present, and cannot change the past. Think of the present as a birthday gift to be unwrapped and enjoyed. Mindercise with a present focus builds your Positive Power.

Helen's Story

Helen is an intelligent and experienced administrator in the field of healthcare. Because of her aptitude and efficiency, her superiors at corporate headquarters elected to give her a sizable bonus. When the bonus was entered into the payroll system, there was a negative reaction from members of the medical staff, who felt she should have dispersed some of the money to the employees. And they told her so. Helen's first reaction was to feel badly, to engage in self-blame, and to feel responsible for creating problems.

She felt greedy, uncomfortable, and unworthy for the differential bonus. Of course, Helen was responsible for her superior work, not the corporate bonus decision. Upset, worried, and contrite, Helen discussed the bonus situation with her support network, which is comprised of both women and men. The women agonized with her. The men were incredulous: "How come you are not thrilled? This is a case of sour grapes. This is the reality of the evolution of medical practices to incorporate business practices. In the corporate culture, administrative bonuses are specific to the individual and appropriate."

Once Helen was able to look at the issue from a broader perspective, she was able to change her self-talk and enjoy her bonus. Her initial instinct to criticize herself and feel responsible for her employees evolved into accepting her accomplishments and enjoying her Positive Power.

Affirmations

- Remember the wisdom of Eleanor Roosevelt: No one can make you feel inferior without your consent.
- I am a worthwhile person.
- I can do anything I set my mind to.
- I recognize that my thoughts create my feelings.
- I affirm myself daily.
- I am the captain of my own cheerleading team.
- I am committed to liking myself and accepting myself.
- Attitude is important, and I see the glass as half full.
- I engage in daily mindercise and physical exercise.

POSITIVE POWER LESSON #5
I need to ask for what I want to reach my goals.

Questions to Ask Yourself

- Do you assume full responsibility for creating opportunity in your life?
- Do you no longer need to ask permission to make requests?
- Are you comfortable making direct requests?
- Do you know what you want?
- Do you have a life strategy?

Moving Beyond

Power Up training requires going beyond politely asking for permission straight to assuming personal responsibility for creating what you want in life. You become the designer and sculptor of your life. You assume a Positive Power position to control the outcome of your life. You no longer ask permission or depend on others for the opportunities you need. Instead, voice your requests directly. Become an activist in your own life and create opportunities as the moments arise.

Asking directly for what you want requires that you know what you want. Often women spend so much time fulfilling the needs and desires of others, they neglect identifying their own goals. Given women's powerful socialization training, this "other focus" is understandable. You now need to develop a strong internal focus, which allows you to identify your own personal goals and needs. Once you have completed the identification process, you then begin to develop and implement a plan to reach your goals.

Much like a butterfly sheds its cocoon, you begin to discard the past behaviors of indirectness and asking permission. As you identify and create new paths of opportunity in your life, you discover the shortest route between two places is always the most direct route. Your focus is to be direct, expedient, and to create opportunities. You discard the expectation of someone else taking care of you, and assume responsibilities while creating opportunities.

Emma's Story

Emma is a 24-year-old who works at a medical supply sales company in Austin, Texas. She has been with the company for ten months and has excelled in training and selling company products to current and new clients. Her supervisor noted her professional success in the office and Emma was asked to travel more frequently on behalf of the company.

Traveling to different conferences allowed Emma the opportunity to network with a variety of doctors, nurses, and hospital executives to introduce and sell her company's medical supplies. Emma discovered her personable and extroverted personality provided a successful foundation for professional success. Emma became a key member of her company's sales team, bringing in a consistent portfolio of new clients monthly and maintaining positive professional relationships with current clients. When Emma was first hired, her employment contract gave her a base salary, which was sufficient at the time for her work; however, her new role called for a renegotiation of her employment contract. Emma recognized her work increased company profits. She knew she would not be able to reach her goals without directly asking and negotiating her base salary plus commission benefits with her supervisor. Emma wanted to seize this opportunity but knew she would have to ask.

Instead of asking casually during a workday, Emma arranged a meeting with her supervisor to discuss job performance close to the one-year anniversary of her start date. Emma prepared a presentation for her supervisor including empirical data and tangible results of her sales for the company. She made the salary request and negotiated commission parameters. Her "ask" was professional and prepared. It allowed her supervisor the opportunity to truly see the impact of Emma's work on the company. Emma's supervisor agreed to raising her salary and opening commission opportunities in her employment contact. Emma learned that good work can go unnoticed and to succeed in life people can reach their potential by asking for what they want.

Affirmations

- People cannot read my mind; I must say what I want.
- I want to maximize the possibility of reaching my goals.
- I am responsible for getting what I need.
- If I ask directly, I increase the possibility of having my request fulfilled.
- By asking clearly and directly, I am an effective communicator.
- I need to consistently plan and reassess my life goals.
- I seize opportunities to reach my goals.

5

Advanced Power Robbers Awareness

"Creative minds have always been known to survive any kind of bad training."

— Anna Freud, Psychoanalyst

Stop the Power Drain

As we discussed in chapter 3, power robber behaviors quietly sneak into our behavioral repertoire without our awareness. No one consciously gives away his or her power. It is a sequence of subtle events that can undermine our personal effectiveness. This chapter continues to raise your awareness and helps you stop your power drain. Power robbers are to be monitored. We cannot totally eliminate these socially ingrained behaviors. However, an increased awareness can minimize their impact on your life. You can reduce the "power drain." Get ready to take the next step to power up!

POWER ROBBER #6
I want others to like me.

Messages From Society

- What others think about you is important.
- You grow and blossom with compliments from others.
- People who have high opinions of themselves are arrogant and pompous.
- Valuing yourself is being selfish.

Questions to Ask Yourself

- Do you look carefully at the body language of others before you make a statement?
- Do you get upset if someone tells you someone else does not like you?
- Do you go out of your way to curry favor with others?
- Do you keep your opinion to yourself because you want to be liked by others?
- Do you play over and over in your head criticism made by others?

Isabella's Story

Isabella is a midcareer entrepreneur who owns a frozen yogurt franchise. She decided to open a second shop in New England. After extensive research, she chose a location along the seacoast in Portsmouth, New Hampshire, which is a recently rediscovered sailor's haunt and now a popular business destination. Her first step — check out the local women's Chamber of Commerce.

There were two ice cream shops and one other yogurt shop in Portsmouth. Isabella did not realize that one of the ice cream shops and the yogurt shop both were women-owned. At the first breakfast meeting, Isabella was warmly greeted and several women introduced themselves. However, when she entered the main room, there was an audible gasp from Leah, who owned the other yogurt shop and a rather chilly glare from Annette, owner of the ice cream shop.

Isabella sat at a table with two other members and introduced herself. Her heart was beating fast, and she felt her face getting red. She noticed that at Leah's and Annette's tables there were whispered conversations and long glances aimed in her direction. She felt very uncomfortable.

After the breakfast and before the speaker, Isabella went to the ladies room. From behind the bathroom stall, she overheard two women whom she did not know talking. One said to the other, "It's refreshing to have a newcomer in our group, and Isabella seems like a pleasant person." The other woman replied, "It will be interesting to see what kind of a person she is." Isabella wondered whether she should leave or stay. Her instinct was to leave.

Isabella overcame her discomfort and got involved. Six months later, she was asked to serve on the membership committee. Isabella was congenial and accepting of both Annette and Leah. Soon Leah stopped attending Chamber meetings. Isabella and Annette became friendly. And as Isabella marked her first year in Portsmouth, she and Annette were considering cross promoting the ice cream shop and the yogurt shop. Isabella rejected the power robber of worrying about upsetting others by remaining with the organization and committing to its success. Clearly, focusing on your own worth and not letting others deter you is important for "powering up!"

Overview

Acceptance and popularity can be traps. If you focus on what others are thinking, you cannot follow your own path. Being popular, being elected Prom Queen or Most Popular in the Class were badges of honor in high school — a validation of stature and attractiveness.

As women grew up, they were taught to dress and speak to "fit in" and be liked. Your parents emphasized being likeable — that acceptance was good. The worst thing in life was to be considered an outsider, someone shunned by others.

Focusing on opinions of others relinquishes your Positive Power. If the acceptance of others becomes the goal, you live your life to someone else's standards not your own. It is never truly achievable, as it is impossible to be all things to all people. It is difficult and exhausting. Worse, it does not allow you to be true to yourself.

Acceptance and popularity are secondary to your own goals of learning to become your own person. You need to decide what is important in YOUR life. Living by others' standards does not yield a happy and fulfilling life.

Counter Thoughts

- It is important to develop my own goals based on my values and priorities.
- I am respectful of others, but do not let them control my actions.
- I determine my own actions.
- Popularity is fleeting. Living an authentic life is permanent.
- The most important perception is the perception I have of myself.
- No one has the power to diminish my personal value.

POWER ROBBER #7
I need to obey the rules.

Messages From Society

- Good girls obey at all times.
- If you are a lady, you will follow the rules.
- Acting proper is important.
- Girls don't make a mess.
- Following the rules leads to success.

Questions to Ask Yourself

- Do you ever question the sensibility of rules?
- Do you never allow yourself to make an exception to the rules?
- Is being viewed as obedient important to you?
- When deviating from the rules, do you feel guilty?

Olivia's Story

Olivia developed a passion for computer science and technology at an early age. Her interests led her to pursue a degree and eventually a career in technology. She landed her first job at a start-up in Silicon Valley. Similar to the computer software she programmed every day, Olivia's structured and methodical personality enabled her safe and obedient behaviors. Even though she excelled professionally, she did so quietly, never asking for a raise and always waiting to be acknowledged for her successful job performance.

Olivia worked for five-and-a-half years and never took the initiative on projects or sought innovative solutions for workplace problems. She was simply a consistent and safe employee who could be counted on to complete her tasks. Even when the company announced a new office or project launch, Olivia would be indecisive, convincing herself that she lacked the proper experience and education for the position. Maybe someone else was "better" qualified. When in reality, her ability to learn and incorporate her past professional experiences provided her with a solid foundation for any leadership role.

Olivia continues to struggle between following the rules and stretching her wings. When you obey the rules with blind acceptance, you limit your full potential. Olivia's rule-following mentality limits her personal growth and professional success. She is content doing her job but lacks an innovative spirit. Would Olivia be in a managerial position if she took more initiative? Is she limiting her future success?

When a new position was posted for project director of new software, Olivia was approached by the vice president and asked to apply. The encouragement from management tipped the scales, and Olivia stepped outside her comfort zone and applied for the position. She was chosen as project director.

Overview

Rule-following women hold themselves back in life by accepting stereotypical behaviors they've been taught since childhood. From an early age, we are subtly taught that being "nice" is more important than getting what we truly want. As a result, we sabotage our personal and professional relationships and fail to reach our full potential.

Gender rules on obedience are flagrantly different. The tolerance for boys to be naughty and mischievous is dramatically high. The expectation that "boys will be boys," is prevalent in society. Boys naturally disobey to "test their limits." However, minimal tolerance exists for acting-out behaviors for girls. Girls are expected to walk a narrow line. If a girl is not acting in an acceptable manner, she is immediately labeled a tomboy and looked at with dismay. Even in the classroom, teachers tolerate boys yelling out their answers. However, it is important girls raise their hands and wait to be acknowledged. This programming to be obedient and wait to be acknowledged will result in your waiting your whole life to get what you want.

Blind obedience to the rules makes it difficult for women to engage in meaningful negotiations. Rule following may cause you to assume that the only response to a request is to automatically meet it, rather than negotiate. A strong adherence to rules limits opportunity, making flexible and creative responses difficult. Remember, outrageous, rule-breaking decisions may lead to phenomenal success!

Counter Thoughts

- Rules cannot cover all circumstances.
- Rules need to be bent to fit the situation.
- Rules can be creatively applied.
- For every rule, there is an exception.

POWER ROBBER #8
I need to treat everyone equally.

Messages From Society

- Watch out — be sure to be fair.
- You need to treat everyone equally.
- You wouldn't want to be left out — be sure you include everyone.
- Don't show favoritism.

Questions to Ask Yourself

- Do you find yourself carefully evaluating how much time you spend with each of your friends?
- Do you find yourself worrying about whether you are spending as much money on a gift for one person as you did for another?

- Do you find yourself being concerned that someone might think you an "apple polisher" who is paying too much attention to upper management?
- Do you find yourself worrying about being fair in the office?
- Do you often say life is not fair?

Lily's Story

Lily has been in the boutique business for fifteen years. Previously, she was an editor at a fashion publication. Lily started her own chapter of Business Network International (BNI), acknowledging that she wanted to be viewed as fair and just. "I am very concerned with others' judgment of me." As the discussion continued, Lily related her conflicted emotions with the realities of being a business owner. She stated, "I go above and beyond for major customers, because they are the ones contributing the most to my bottom line. Although I strive to give superior service to all my customers, the reality is I cannot provide the same level of service to everyone."

Lily also discussed the difficulty of balancing fairness with conflicting demands of employees. Inevitably, one employee will ask for special favors. In most companies, seniority is perceived as a factor in making requests; however, Lily feels compelled to consider the impact such perceived favoritism has on other employees. Her constant concern with fairness and equal treatment generates added pressure. Lily personifies the struggles of a businesswoman who has to base her decisions on economic realities, not relationships.

As her BNI chapter grew, Lily began to recognize that business owners needed to engage in a cost-benefit analysis both with customers and employees. Decision-making needed to be based on contributions to the bottom line **not** fairness or equality. Slowly, she began to eliminate her guilt, adjust her fairness guideline and recognize the economic realities of business and life decision-making.

Overview

Women appear to be imbued with an idealistic view that if you treat others fairly, people will treat you fairly. In addition to believing in the "reciprocal fairness" theory, women also believe that fairness is essential. However, in many ways, fairness is a subjective perception. The reality of life is sometimes different. You want to be supportive of others, but you need to consider carefully the dangers of not individualizing your interactions with others. If you believe in the idea of fair and equal treatment to everyone — independent of productivity, independent of what a customer may add to the bottom line, independent of the reciprocal benefits — it will be difficult for you to lead or be adequately effective in your life.

Many business and personal situations exist where differential treatment has to be considered. The fairness theory leaves you vulnerable to power drains of energy. If you continue to accommodate everyone equally, you are not preserving your energy. You need to consider the reciprocity of your relationships, and invest your energies in relationships where reciprocity and benefits exist.

The concept of "equality for fairness" also presents problems in terms of time. If you treat everyone equally, you are going to give away the precious commodity of time because you are going to speak to everyone equally. Particularly in terms of time management, you will find it is essential to make assessments to maintain your own productivity and control over your time. Time is not a commodity you can purchase or recover.

While we certainly need to recognize that consideration of others is essential, fairness and equal treatment should only be *part* of the variables in your decision-making equation. Adequate decision-making must include an assessment of time variables, productivity variables, financial variables, reciprocity variables, and benefits. People with effective power consider all the variables and make decisions accordingly. Women need to recognize we have to fairly assess all variables, and then move forward.

Counter Thoughts

- Different people add differently to my life.
- Different circumstances need to be responded to with different behaviors.
- Life is not a neat process where everything can be meted out in equal measure.
- Each situation must be evaluated independently with consideration of many variables.

POWER ROBBER #9

I must keep the peace and not make waves.

Messages From Society

- Don't speak unless you are spoken to.
- Be respectful — don't contradict.
- Girls should be seen and not heard.
- Don't be a troublemaker.

Questions to Ask Yourself

- Do you view yourself as a peacemaker?
- Do you have difficulty "speaking out?"
- Is it difficult for you to express a different point of view?
- Do you prefer to be in the background rather than the forefront?
- Do you see being a wavemaker as being a troublemaker?

Heather's Story

Heather's parents, especially her father, subscribe to old-world thinking regarding women, privacy, and traditional values. Heather, who always kept the peace in her home by doing what she was told and accepting others' decisions, found herself in a predicament. She was unhappy in her position as a probation officer, and while the job was secure, she found it depressing and frustrating. She began to feel sad, unmotivated, drained. One of her friends recommended a therapist. Heather's parents, who felt she should not make waves at her job, and under no circumstances, should she air her troubles to a "stranger," cautioned against making changes or seeking help.

During this uncertain time for Heather, her family returned to their native Spain to live. The absence of her parents in her day-to-day life made it easier for Heather to enter therapy. She was pleased with the therapist's focus on here-and-now life strategies as opposed to a focus on her childhood and past. With new tools in her skill set and the freedom to pursue what suited *her*, instead of her parents, Heather began searching for different job opportunities. Six months later, she accepted a sales position with a distributor of pet food supplies. Always a pet lover, her enthusiasm for her job helped increase her sales and raise her happiness quotient.

Today, Heather is more vocal and assertive. However, she still hears her father's voice when she attempts something new. By keeping the power robbers at bay by engaging in counter thinking, Heather is learning to expand her Positive Power skills and blaze her own trail. She makes time for therapeutic life coaching and continues to remodel her life.

Overview

Females typically play the role of peacemaker. The difficulty with being a peacemaker is that you constantly seek agreement, which results in losing the opportunity to ask provocative questions. If you are afraid of making waves, it undermines your ability to make a strong impression. The idea of women needing to suppress themselves has even been popularized in the media. Remember Edith and Archie Bunker? Archie repeatedly told Edith to "stifle yourself." Stifling yourself is an extremely power-draining behavior. Camille Paglia states in her groundbreaking book, *Vamps and Tramps*, "The 'nice' girl with her soft, sanitized speech and decorous manners, had to go."

Messages to avoid contrary opinions have been communicated to women for more than two hundred years. Remember, avoiding wave-making hampers growth and occurs when peace at all costs represses constructive conflict. Using constructive conflict allows you to challenge traditional viewpoints and respond to change more effectively. Particularly in these times, active involvement as an agent of change is essential.

Strong influences often prevent women from being wavemakers. Characterizing a woman as a "bitch" is often society's attempt to keep her in line. Additionally, women often resist "speaking out," not because of stage fright but rather fear of retribution. Remember, during the Puritan witch-hunts, an expression of contrary opinions could cost women their lives.

In early American history, women who spoke up would be chastised publicly for displaying such assertiveness. In this way, the subtle socialization of controlling women's verbalizations became engrained in society.

Deborah Tannen notes in her book, *You Just Don't Understand: Women and Men in Conversation,* that women often engage in assenting behaviors that mask their expertise and cause them to avoid mobilizing their talents as a source of power. Leadership requires decisiveness and "making waves." Managers, entrepreneurs, community leaders, and parents all need to respond to change with creativity and input. You want your insight to be included in the information used for decision-making. Women frequently have a unique perspective that enhances decisions. Allow your voice to be heard. Make waves!

Counter Thoughts

- Having a different opinion is not adversarial.
- I can be considerate and respectful while still expressing my opinion.

- Expressing an opinion and taking a stand is necessary for women's wisdom to have an impact.
- All conflict is not to be avoided.
- Varying perspectives from women and men enhance decisions.

POWER ROBBER #10

I must wait to be recognized for my achievements.

Messages From Society

- It is not appropriate for women to brag.
- Be careful to wait your turn.
- Ladies don't draw attention to themselves.
- Don't be too smart; you will create problems.
- Give credit to others before yourself.

Questions to Ask Yourself

- Do you expect that recognition will only come as a result of fine work?
- Do you rely on the awareness of others to recognize your achievements?
- Do you feel it is bragging to talk about your achievements?
- Do you compliment others without recognizing your achievements?

Patricia's Story

Patricia has been an outstanding regional manager for more than nine years. Presently she manages more than sixty salespeople. Despite her achievements, Patricia has difficulty calling attention to the successes of her team. She states, "I don't call the vice president and tell him about our latest contract. I just assume he'll notice it when the monthly sales figures are reported." As a result, Patricia and her team go unrecognized while other managers are acknowledged and compensated to a greater degree.

Patricia's MO is to finish one major sales presentation and move on to the next, without sharing the details of her team's latest success with others — especially the higher-ups. This behavior virtually ensures her compensation will not keep pace with her achievements. When she contrasts her behavior with that of the male managers, she admits they provide blow-by-blow descriptions of their sales team's accomplishments, and position themselves as "knights in shining armor."

Patricia is increasingly aware that her reluctance to call attention to her accomplishments is self-limiting. As aggressively as she works and recognizes her team members, she is still learning how to be an advocate for herself. Until she connects the dots and increases her "up-line" communication, she won't be adequately compensated.

Overview

Women's subtle socialization messages are directed at diminishing their achievements. Rather than accepting recognition, do you find yourself saying: "Oh, it was nothing," or "I was just in the right place at the right time," or "It didn't take that much work," or "It was really due to the team or my boss."

Researchers report definite gender difference in credit-taking behaviors. When men succeed, they take the credit fully. When men fail, they point to external variables. When women fail, they self-criticize and tend to take the blame. And when they succeed, they're either mum about it or deflect acknowledgement. The gender behaviors of women and men in describing success and failure are opposite. The propensity to be self-critical and not take credit for a job well done robs you of the joy that comes from achieving goals, and diminishes your self-esteem.

In a 2013 interview on CNBC, Shirley Davis, vice president of diversity and inclusion at the Society for Human Resource Management, said, "women tend to be less likely to tout their own accomplishments on a regular basis in staff meetings or one-on-one. Those reminders can prime the pump for asking for a raise later."

Women have to be aware of the "depressed entitlement effect." This behavior is often found among minorities — including women — who devalue themselves when compared to others. Many studies indicate that devaluing achievements is a major contribution to the wage gap between the genders. Women need to move beyond self-effacing behaviors. They need to accept credit and draw attention to their achievements. The fact is: Women are no longer a minority. We make up 51 percent of the United States' population, which gives us the power of the majority; plus, we currently outnumber males seeking postgraduate degrees, and by 2022, will make up 56 percent of the workforce.

We have been cajoled, and sometimes bullied, into keeping a low profile. It's time we expand our comfort level to become comfortable with a higher profile. If you do not create visibility, there is no way for your work to be noticed and opportunities to be created. You are endowed by nature with the ability to achieve outstanding accomplishments — your challenge is to identify areas where you shine, and then channel your energies and abilities into mastering them.

Internalizing praise and accepting recognition is essential to the acquisition of Positive Power. If you wait to be recognized, you wind up in a holding pattern, much like waiting to be asked out on a date. This antiquated behavior strips you of your ability to take the initiative and have control over your life. One thing to guard against, however, is going from undervaluing your accomplishments to feeling entitled. Letting your accomplishments be recognized is not obnoxious or overbearing — it is simply taking appropriate, earned credit. Wait until you experience how exhilarating it is when you let your "star power" shine!

Counter Thoughts

- I am responsible for commendable work and creating opportunities for acknowledgement.
- Bragging and acknowledging are two different behaviors.

- I strive to accept compliments without minimizing behaviors.
- I am committed to appropriately accepting credit and giving credit to others.

Controlling Power Robbers

As is evident, all women experience power robber messages. It's true, few messages are black and white, and avoiding polarity-thinking means you do not eliminate every message. It's important to sift through messages and extract important values, like respect and interacting with sensitivity and caring to others.

The most effective way to control power-robbing thoughts is to practice counter thoughts. Since our thoughts control our beliefs, which, in turn, control our actions, women must include both situational variables and those of their needs, wants, and goals. You need to ensure that your concerns are adequately represented as you engage in your daily activities. By controlling the power robbers in your life, you gain control of your future.

Each of us needs to recognize that power robbers are never fully eliminated. Each power robber needs to be monitored and countered. As each of us stops the power drain, we charge up to save our energy to engage new power tools.

6

Charging It Up: Advanced Positive Power Lessons

"I do not wish women to have power over men; but over themselves."

— Mary Wollstonecraft, Feminist Author

Charging Up Your Life

Ready for more power tools? You began establishing a foundation of Positive Power behaviors in chapter 4. Let's keep the momentum going by exploring the advanced power lessons in chapter 6. Positive Power skills are the key to navigating your life. Each of us needs to create new cognitive templates to guide our behavior so we can power up to the next level.

POSITIVE POWER LESSON #6
I am centered and value myself.

Questions to Ask Yourself

- Am I willing to accept total responsibility for my welfare?
- Do I enjoy my relationships versus being dependent on my relationships?
- Do I seek opportunities to develop my abilities?
- Do I find that my ability to be self-sufficient is an exciting prospect?

Moving Beyond

Allowing yourself to focus on your abilities and talents creates *internal* security. When you remain *externally* focused on relationships as essential to life function, you are doomed to a rollercoaster of worry and insecurity. Women have strong needs for affiliation. While associations are enjoyable, remember the one person you need to rely on is yourself. Self-reliance and self-sufficiency are key to maintaining adequate equilibrium and being in charge of your life.

Security in life stems from having varied abilities and multiple skills as your core competencies. As a competent individual, you recognize and develop your talents. You have the ability to earn a living and you have the ability to reach out to tap needed resources. Your security arises from the recognition of your strengths, your talents, and your abilities. Being able to acknowledge and recognize your talents and abilities also allows you to acknowledge your successes.

Confident individuals focus on building their strengths and widening their core competencies while minimizing their limitations. Recognizing and accepting personal responsibility for your economic, emotional, and social life, brings a motivating freedom to expand your skills. You become committed to the expansion of your core competencies to create your preferred lifestyle. Self-sufficiency and self-reliance do not limit your ability to enjoy relationships, recognize the importance of interpersonal interactions, or treasure loved ones. Internal security allows you to enjoy people for what they add to your life, rather than for what they can do for you. Interpersonal relationships become more joyous and open without hidden dependency agendas.

The security you acquire in life is through your efforts. Security is when you have effective life strategies and the ability to traverse life with confidence, multiple strategies, and resources through your core competencies.

Rachel's Story

Rachel started "Dynamite Hair" in her forties. Now, in her sixties, she wants to work fewer hours and has decided to groom Samantha, a talented stylist with an MBA, to take over her thriving business. Three other stylists also work at the salon as independent contractors. As is common in the salon trade, the owner provides the shop and referrals as well as marketing. The stylists "rent" their chairs.

Rachel and Samantha developed a long-term business plan that included relocating the salon to a bigger, better location. Together, they found a more contemporary space with plenty of parking and negotiated the lease. Rachel invested more than $20,000 to ensure the new salon would appeal to a broader clientele.

Rachel met one on one with each of her stylists to talk over the new location and eventual sale of the business to Samantha. She also discussed a modest increase in the "rent" each would have to pay, because of the new salon's higher overhead costs. (This was also Rachel's way of ensuring there was adequate cash flow when Samantha took over the business.) Rachel explained that the new location was certain to draw more clients, which would more than compensate for the increase in the chair rental fee. Everyone was onboard with the proposed changes.

Six months after the move, Rachel and Samantha hosted a well-attended grand opening. Shortly after, Rachel raised the monthly chair rental fee 2 percent. Rachel was stunned when two of the stylists asked, "Why is there an increase in the overhead?" Within six months all three stylists resigned.

Attempts to negotiate with the stylists failed. Clearly, they were resentful of the changes. However, Rachel and Samantha had enough confidence in their business plan and strategic goals to let them go. Despite a short-term increase in expenses for Rachel, she knew selling the business to Samantha was the best long-term goal. Both recognized they were in a desirable location and offered a convivial work environment where talented stylists could thrive. All they needed to do was stay the course.

Within weeks, two new stylists were at their stations taking care of clients. Today, Rachel works as many — or as few — hours as she wants. Samantha has slipped into the managerial role with relish and five independent stylists now call Dynamite Hair home.

Rachel and Samantha set high standards, showed resilience and are thriving! **Having clarity of your self-worth boosts your Positive Power. Recognizing the value of your business acumen is essential to maintaining quality in your life.**

Affirmations

- My relationships are only a portion of my life, and I am independently capable.
- I can set meaningful goals that give direction to my life.

- I can choose what I want and go after it.
- I can ask for help when I need it.
- I can be flexible and persistent in pursuing my goals.
- I recognize and develop my talents.

POSITIVE POWER LESSON #7
I need to understand the rules and be flexible.

Questions to Ask Yourself

- Do you reevaluate policies and procedures on a regular basis?
- Do you allow exceptions to the rules?
- Do you take the time to flex a policy when necessary?
- Are you comfortable challenging rules that appear inappropriate?
- Is it more important for you to solve the problem rather than follow the rules?

Moving Beyond

The world would be chaotic if rules were not present. However, a respect for rules does not preclude the need for flexibility. At times, challenging a rule is appropriate. Rules generally are broad stokes that cannot possibly anticipate every situation. Consequently, each situation demands a close examination of the rules, and may require occasional flexing. To be effective, you have to possess the flexibility to modify a response. Be astute in your application of rules and understand there most likely will be exceptions. Be sensitive to individual cases and don't sabotage yourself or alienate others by blindly adhering to the rules. You might want to think of rules as more like guidelines.

In many organizations, there exists a "shadow organization" or an informal power line. Understanding informal power and the presence of unwritten rules is essential to effective functioning. Both written and unwritten rules need to be evaluated before determining a course of action.

To be successful, you need to see beyond the rules or even create a new set of rules. Innovative flexibility is an indispensible power tool when it comes to developing new visions and activating change. It is particularly crucial for women as they are challenged to use their power and wisdom to reshape the world.

Amy's Story

Amy is a recruiter for a technology company. She is familiar with the company's hiring objectives and goals, and knows the principals of the company prefer candidates with a degree in computer science. They believe that a formal education produces the most productive and successful employees.

One day Amy received a call from a major client who asked if she would interview a highly qualified candidate for a job. Even though the individual did not have a strong background in technology, Amy agreed to interview her based on the client's recommendation and out of respect for the relationship with her company.

During the interview, Amy was impressed with the woman's professional presence and vision. Plus, she'd done her homework and was able to present fresh ideas and a relevant business model that would enable Amy's company to work more efficiently and expand their consumer markets.

The main impediment: The applicant specialized in business development and only had a passing interest in technology. Amy worried about the strict parameters her company had set. In the past, she had always followed the employment guidelines — playing it safe on every hire she made. This time was different. Amy recognized the potential and value this recruit could bring to the company. But, she struggled with the "rules." She knew she could not hire this individual without speaking to the principals.

Amy weighed her decision. It would be risky to challenge the hiring policy, but it could also be her first opportunity to act as an agent of change within the company. So, Amy scheduled a meeting with the board of directors and managing staff to brief them on the candidate's potential hire, even offering a second interview to select members. Her supervisors were open to a second interview, which was a positive first step in challenging the company's strict hiring procedures. Amy was commended for her willingness to bend the rules and bring a superior talent to the attention of upper management.

Affirmations

- I recognize that rules may become outdated.
- I respect the rules but know they need to be challenged at times.
- I value my ability to be flexible and conduct a situational analysis.
- I have the ability to question rules and make needed changes.
- People are more important than rules.
- I consider both written and unwritten rules in my decision-making.
- I choose to be a change agent and establish new rules, when appropriate.

POSITIVE POWER LESSON #8
I need to be discriminating in my interactions with others.

Questions to Ask Yourself

- Do you carefully consider your resources before volunteering for a committee?
- Do you think carefully before automatically accepting projects?
- Do you select among invitations?
- Do you take time to evaluate the reciprocity of relationships?
- Have you developed criteria for the type of collegial support you need to advance toward your goals?

Moving Beyond

Time and energy are limited. As a consequence, it is important for you to be highly discriminating in your interactions with others. The best investments of time and energy are when you make selections that bring benefits into your life. By making differential assessments, you are able to establish priorities and meet goals. If you are constantly available and consistently spread yourself equally among relationships, you will not have the focus or the time to reach your goals.

Develop a support team. Choose people with diverse and complementary skills and strengths. Use your Positive Power to identify alliances that will enhance your life, and then invite them into your circle.

Connectedness is important. Psychological studies demonstrate that human interaction is essential to the quality of life. Even as an infant, the absence of human touch and interaction can result in a "failure to thrive." Human connections are precious and to be treasured. Since time is limited, it is important to choose your alliances carefully. Align yourself with people who are life enhancing and supportive. Taking time to assess your relationships and ensure adequate reciprocity is a powerful way to honor yourself.

Madeline's Story

Madeline is a 30-year-old event planner who built her business by working hard, being detail-oriented, extremely creative and, oftentimes, underpaid. After seven years, she enjoyed an excellent reputation in the community for the innovative events she planned. But, while Madeline succeeded creatively, she struggled financially.

She discussed her business challenges with her women's entrepreneur group and admitted she rarely factored the time she spent into the fees she charged clients for her services. Her colleagues recommended she analyze her time, the costs and compensation of each event.

After the meeting, Madeline compared her time investment to the financial compensation she earned from the events and realized she was undervaluing her contributions. She began to factor in her costs as well as consistent compensation for herself. She hired an intern to help coordinate the details, thus freeing her to spend time with clients and focus on the big picture.

Madeline became more discriminating of her time, and began to work smarter, rather than harder. By wisely investing her physical and emotional energy, her feelings of being overwhelmed decreased and her bottom line increased. Plus, she had the distinct satisfaction that comes from mentoring someone.

Affirmations

- I must carefully invest my time.
- I must wisely invest my physical and emotional energies.
- I make discriminating use of time and energy to increase my quality of living.
- By being discriminating, I have adequate time for self-care.
- I reserve my time for people who are most important to me.
- I develop alliances that benefit me.

POSITIVE POWER LESSON #9
I want to makes waves and be a change catalyst.

Questions to Ask Yourself

- Do you create opportunities to take the initiative?
- Do you enjoy being a pivotal member of an organization?
- Do you view yourself as having unique perspectives that will be of major benefit to an organization?
- Are you willing to take a stand that is different from others in the management team?
- Are you able to develop your own unique vision and goals for the organization?

Moving Beyond

Talent inspires productivity. Releasing your talent contributes to your organization's growth and your expression of Positive Power. Stifling yourself through fear of being called the "B" word limits your ability to contribute and achieve, and robs the organization of your valuable insight. You're a talented individual. Don't stand on the sidelines; get in the game. Get involved. Take your foot off your power brake, speak out, and seize the initiative.

Initiative occurs along with an overpowering urge for action and is crucial to forward momentum. When you are an initiator, you are a pivotal person. Group performance pivots around action people. So, when you take the initiative and speak out, you are viewed as a seasoned player whose comments are worthy of consideration. This is a lesson women must learn, because women have been socialized to defer, not lead.

Leadership and initiative allow you to become an effective change agent. Women with their unique ways of knowing as well as their considerable talents have much to contribute to businesses as entrepreneurs and to corporate cultures as executives. Failure to use 100 percent of the workforce talent, by excluding women's contributions, greatly affects the bottom line and hampers business growth.

Today, women are primed by the critical mass of numbers to be agents of transformation. We have been in the ranks long enough to take leadership positions. When one is a valued senior manager, you speak the truth about business realities and make important contributions to the directions of business. And people listen.

Research demonstrates that executive women in upper management and those who own their own companies are more likely to address business challenges openly, make the necessary waves, and implement changes. Women who conform to the norm and avoid the initiative are not using the full spectrum of their Positive Power. Moreover, women with their unique ways of knowing have perceptive abilities different from men — expressing these unique insights assists the change process.

Learn to be out in front and take the initiative. Express your unique perspectives, and change things. As a catalyst of change, you will discover your alliances will strengthen, because others are drawn to those who possess a vision and offer new ideas.

Jacqueline's Story

Jacqueline, a 51-year-old mother of three, married at nineteen to escape an abusive stepfather. Her dreams and expectations of marriage were blissful. She wanted to be an ideal housewife who cared for her home, children, and husband. As the years passed, she began to recognize how alike her husband was to her stepfather. He often criticized and belittled her. Nothing she did was ever right or good enough.

Years later her stepfather died. The day she returned from the funeral, Mary looked at her husband, gathered her courage and said "I'm ready to start a new chapter in my life. I want a divorce." At first, her children were frantic. They felt she was giving up her security. Jacqueline went forward with the divorce and joined a divorce support group.

At one of the support group meetings, she met two women who were attending a charity event for a Center for Abused Women. She joined them and subsequently volunteered at the Center and began to attend college at night. For the first time in years, Jacqueline felt she was part of the changing role of women.

The Center expanded and posted a new position for a Development Coordinator. Jacqueline had finished her degree and, once again, took the initiative and applied for the position. She is now a valued member of the management team.

Affirmations

- I have a unique perspective that needs to be expressed.
- Being a change agent adds meaning to my life.
- I enjoy the challenge of moving an organization in new directions.

- As a change agent, I maintain critical alliances.
- Taking initiative is crucial to reaching my goals.
- Taking initiative allows me to shape the organization toward my vision.

POSITIVE POWER LESSON #10
I acknowledge my accomplishments and seek appropriate recognition.

Questions to Ask Yourself

- Do you acknowledge your significant contributions to a project?
- Do you create opportunities for broadening your achievements by expanding your skills?
- Do you accept acknowledgements gracefully without diminishing them?
- Do you seek opportunities to have your achievements communicated?

Moving Beyond

Prior messages to keep a low profile and stay in the background counteract your ability to obtain recognition and acknowledgement for your accomplishments. Obtaining recognition is necessary to create new opportunities. Having Positive Power and handling it with ease requires that you receive acknowledgements comfortably. In addition, you need to create a comprehensive record of your achievements and leadership roles to move even further forward.

Acknowledging accomplishments and seeking appropriate avenues for recognition are necessary steps in climbing the ladder of success. Identifying appropriate avenues to seek recognition requires that you be a strategic listener. You always want to engage in active listening, possess a good memory for names (or find a recall tool), and be viewed as considerate and credible.

Seeking acknowledgement is not being egotistical; rather, it shows respect and appreciation for yourself and others. You follow up strategic listening with speedy responses that include suggestions. You send thank-you notes with an exchange of ideas. You develop deep down feelings of your own self-worth and you possess a positive self-image. You take pride in what you do and what you are accomplishing.

Establishing credibility and integrity is essential to boosting your profile. Your word is your bond. You say what you're going to do, and then you do it. You enhance your reputation whenever you follow through on a request, keep a promise, and make decisions based on what you support. As you stockpile your accomplishments and raise your profile in the organization, you increase your Positive Power position. You, then, will be viewed as a rainmaker. And, as we all know, rainmakers shape policy and contribute to an organization's vision and bottom line.

Melinda's Story

Melinda is a buyer for a major retail store. During a complex transition to new computers, she often worked sixteen-hour days. Plus, she coached, mentored, and trained a junior, male colleague. She was so involved in the tasks at hand, that she had minimal contact with her managers. And, when she did attempt to meet with them, she found herself being excluded.

What got Melinda's attention was when she received a poor evaluation and was transferred to another store; whereas, the co-worker she mentored received a major raise and was promoted. Clearly, her colleague was more adept at "tooting his horn" than she was.

Up to this point, Melinda had not paid sufficient attention to making upper management aware of her accomplishments and performance. As a salaried employee, she had no tracking mechanism for her efforts, and her manager was not aware of the number of hours she worked or her contribution to her junior colleague's projects.

After several executive-coaching sessions, Melinda appropriately contacted the human resources department regarding her unsatisfactory evaluation, and, subsequently, met with upper management. Only then did they recognize her significant contributions. Despite the company policy of mentoring women managers, management did not "walk the talk" by providing an adequate program.

After the grievance process, Melinda became more conscious of the "recognition factor." She documented her job performance and initiated meetings with her manager. Her initiatives resulted in a letter of commendation and a bonus. In her last session, Melinda stated, "I will never be invisible again. I recognize that communicating your achievements is as important as the achievement itself."

Affirmations

- Acknowledgments are not boasting.
- Recognition creates new opportunities.
- "Tooting my own horn" is necessary for advancement.
- When I acknowledge my achievements, I also can acknowledge others' achievements and strengthen my alliances.
- I seek opportunities to be recognized.
- I recognize that by being acknowledged I position myself as a leader.

Activating the Lessons

In the prior chapter, you raised your awareness of subtle power drains. This chapter continued the development of new skills. We challenge you to tap into the reservoir of power that rests within you. Do not let fear stand in your way. Overcome it by activating your new Positive

Power skills. Althea Horner, in her insightful book, *The Wish for Power and the Fear of Having It*, noted, "Real power transcends the whim of chance or fortune, enabling the individual to preserve and even triumph through adversity." Positive Power skills are keys to opening the doors of increased opportunity.

Power Tools Leveraged

Throughout the research and preparation for this book, personal, collegial, and clinical experience with hundreds of talented women convinced us of the importance of fostering women's perceptions of themselves as powerful, talented, and valuable human beings. This is not, we emphasize, advocating for women to be male-like. Power can be expressed in multiple ways. The Positive Power that is essential to life is a calming power of personal clarity. The nurturing biological template for women gives rise to the potential for you, once you are in touch with your Positive Power, to reshape the world. There is not a single vision to be fulfilled in this reshaping. There are multitudes of possibilities to fulfill your individual vision. Women can be talented sculptors uniquely shaping, guiding, and contributing to the entire picture.

Every woman needs to activate her Positive Power to assist the fluid, ongoing process of reshaping and creating a new sculpted paradigm. Every woman needs to activate her Positive Power, to be all that she can be, for to do less is to shrink from her responsibility to herself and the world at large.

As we promote the increased activation of Positive Power and pursue interlacing power with wisdom for use by women, we recognize that you will continue to be challenged by your own use of power, for even Positive Power needs to be exercised with discretion and wisdom. The ambivalent feelings women experience in relation to power stems from their keen appreciation of the responsibilities of power. We have great confidence in the ability of women to become greater activators of their Positive Power.

7

The Talents of Women

"Women are the real architects of society."

— Harriet Beecher Stowe, Author, Social Critic

How Talented We Are!

Self-acknowledgement

Women are not "one size fits all." Gender roles that place all women at one end of the spectrum opposite men are outdated. Women exist on a continuum and possess many talents and different interests. Women come in all shapes, sizes, and colors. However, women possess some unique characteristics. Women bear children, experience menopause, have more right and left brain connections, and are shaped by a combination of our biology and society. In the words of choreographer Twyla Tharp, "I studied men and adapted myself to their world, I tried to emulate them. Eventually, I realized that I didn't have to 'become' a man to be powerful."

Women are beginning to celebrate being women. Women and men have different perspectives that are both to be appreciated and used. Presently, women's unique ways of knowing have been underutilized in boardrooms, corporations, the public sector, and politics.

Research on the unique talents of women would fill volumes. The purpose of this chapter is not an exhaustive overview of gender research. Rather, it highlights some of the exceptional talents women bring to both their personal and professional lives. We matched the following female talents with the demands of the new global economy in mind. The global economy requires both public and private organizations to stretch in new directions. Women can make significant contributions to this stretching and reengineering to prepare for the future. Women's ways of knowing create extraordinarily savvy businesswomen who are exceptional assets.

Data Gatherers

Although biology is not the sole determiner of behavior, recent advances in cognitive science have increased the understanding of brain functions. Studies demonstrate that women have a larger number of connections between the right- and left-brain hemispheres. The right and left parts of the human brain are connected by the corpus callosum. These extra connections allow you to absorb more information between your brain hemispheres. There is a high probability that what is commonly known as women's intuition stems from these expanded connections between the right and left brain.

As the day-to-day knowledge gathered expands, your brain structure helps you sort the enormous masses of information in today's society. Your increased brain connections allow you to accept a wider range of sensory information. Also, your right- and left-brain exchanges give you an advantage in mastering foreign languages. Women's special skills for foreign languages are a major asset in this global economy.

Gender research reports that women have an increased number of receptor rods and cones in the retina. The increased number of rods and cones allows you to receive a wider arc of visual input. In today's technology-driven society, visual cues are crucial. Your wider peripheral vision allows you to incorporate a larger picture. Since you can physically "see more" you collect more visual data. Your increased personal database of knowledge enhances your decision-making. Your challenge is to translate the data from your physical vision to a vision for the future.

Female socialization assists women in becoming superb data gathers. Women are socialized not to discount emotional feelings. Consequently, we are able to incorporate emotional data with factual data. Women, with their other-focused template, have antennae that gather verbal and nonverbal data. You have an enhanced ability to "read" other people and perceptively gauge multiple parameters of any situation. You key in on voice tones, facial expressions, body posture, and moods. Thus, you provide comprehensive assessments that are valuable components of effective negotiations.

Recognize how valuable your talents are. You have the ability to absorb and sort greater quantities of information, gather more visual data and nonverbal cues, and you have well-honed abilities to sense emotions. Remember, comprehensive information is the key to insightful decisions. As a woman, you possess exceptional data-gathering talents.

Information Sharers

Women often create web-like structures that are useful in today's information age. We like to be at the center and invite input from all sources. Sharing information and seeking more information from others contributes to our abilities to communicate effectively. While a chain of command structure still can be recognized, we tend to easily bridge such structures when the need arises. Women managers are less concerned with titles and cumbersome chains of command.

Women create information webs with numerous lines open to input from others. We focus on being in the middle of things and our connectedness to people facilitates our ability to amass and sort information. Women who are in the midst of the people they manage become conduits for information, rather than information blockers. Females enjoy the spontaneous interruption that not only allows a person-to-person connection, but also creates an opportunity to gather more input.

Women have much less of a focus on the need for status that arises from following protocol or proper channels. Once again, while women can abide lines of command, they can also easily cross over these lines to adapt to changing needs and situations. This openness to input from all sources encourages more frequent brainstorming. Little fear exists that ideas will be co-opted or that concerns will arise from obtaining credit for an idea. Rather, the overriding need to compile effective information leverages the growth of a business. This information-sharing process is helpful in a rapidly changing corporate environment. The quicker an organization can incorporate information, the more responsive and effective it will be. The web communication structure women prefer is an asset in today's global economy.

Flexibility

Women possess strong flexibility skills in both considerations of new ideas and adapting to different circumstances. This ability to be flexible, however, means that most women deplore stuffiness and prefer a more relaxed, flexible atmosphere, and indeed thrive in it. Just as the web pattern of information sharing allows greater information gathering, being flexible encourages this communication. Women's societal role has trained them to be flexible — juggling multiple demands to accomplish several tasks with competing priorities. The flexibility to sense individual needs and tailor managerial styles to employee needs are strengths for women. This ability to spontaneously adapt to changing needs is an important quality for managing diverse workforces.

Women are masters of situational leadership with their well-honed human relation's skills. They adjust their style to the individuals they supervise and the situation in which they find themselves. Our situational flexibility is well suited to the rapidly changing workforce.

Power Sharers

Women also are willing to share power by helping those around them. They enjoy mentoring, teaching, and are comfortable fostering employee growth. Females gain considerable pleasure in being a catalyst for the growth of others. As a result, women are interested in allowing others to succeed and want to create an environment for their success.

Team building and team efforts come naturally to many women. In a team situation, all members contribute value to the project, and the pride in achievement is shared among the people on the team. Our ability to share the glory and acknowledge team involvement creates loyalty and enthusiasm in the workplace and increases employee self-esteem. We are less concerned about who gets the credit; we are much more concerned about the goal being accomplished. Eschewing credit can be a double-edged sword, however, since women need to claim responsibility for their accomplishments in order to advance, even while their focus is more on reaching the goal. Women need to differentiate between sharing the achievement through recognition of the team and obtaining the necessary exposure of being the team motivator and key player in accomplishing the task.

Collaboration

Multiple researchers have found that a woman's preferred way of interacting is in a collaborative manner. We readily allow ourselves to appropriately seek help from others and are comfortable interacting with others. The collaborative style of women creates teamwork and consensus, which is becoming the role model for managing in the global marketplace.

The organizations of the future will be built on the strength of relationships among people, rather than formal channels of authority that have guided most organizations. The management skills of collaboration women possess will be indispensible to the future growth of organizations.

Women shine in their team-building skills. They enjoy fostering cooperation, trust, and mutual respect. Women have the ability to relate to all members of the team as *individuals*, not just technicians. Collaboration requires that everyone be recognized and everyone be respected with impromptu brainstorming; melding diverse information sources gives rise to a strong collaborative style. Creative and innovative work teams can be assembled and held together through strong collaborative leadership. Our collaborative leadership style encourages participation by all, enhances the self-worth of all team members, and creates a nourishing environment for the nonhierarchical flow of information.

Women seek to maintain solid relationships that make teams work more smoothly. Our team leadership style results in our pitching in and doing whatever it takes to move the project along, regardless of rank or hierarchy. Many times, women see their projects almost as a living child, and the overall goal is the well-being of the project and their valuable employees. Women show appreciation for everyone's dedication to the project and readily recognize the importance of small, individual contributions that enable the success of the whole project. Women are comfortable with the networking tools of recognition, and often will send thank-you notes to people who helped them achieve the results.

Win-Win Negotiators

In the past, winning usually meant someone else had to lose. Modern day business practices have recognized the importance of all parties in business negotiations becoming winners to some degree. This is known as a win-win situation. A negotiator can achieve these positive results by focusing on a beneficial solution, rather than gaining advantage over an opponent. Women, with their focus on connectedness and enjoyment of interpersonal interaction, prefer to create an outcome of win-win. Compatible benefits are negotiated for each player. Females are much less invested in the traditional win through ensuring loss to a competitor. Victories are pursued less than accords between involved groups.

Women's openness to creativity and win-win solutions is extremely useful in our rapidly changing economy. Negotiators must bring adaptability and flexibility to the table to achieve a mutually beneficial agreement. In today's merger mania, yesterday's competitor may be tomorrow's colleague. Negotiated agreements can easily create bridges to partnerships.

Women enjoy using their interpersonal skills to create harmonious relationships to reach an agreement. Female empathy promotes seeking a positive outcome with a consideration of the interests of the other parties — negotiating benefits to all sides in a win-win process. An area where women have strength in this process is with the ability to put themselves in their competitor's shoes. Empathy for the impact of the action on others is a negotiating strength.

We also take into consideration the human variables and diverse be-haviors of the parties during negotiations. Our ability to read nonverbal cues and our astuteness in assessing human reaction is a phenomenal strength at the negotiating table. Women seek harmonious accords and are win-win negotiators.

Multitask Wizards

For years, women have been attending to a myriad of work activities, both in the home and at the office. We juggle household tasks, demands of children, needs of spouses, business requirements, and oftentimes obligations to elderly parents. For decades, women have developed well-honed experience in balancing conflicting interests, pacing themselves, and creating incredible organization systems. We are masters at juggling diverse personalities, solving problems, and ensuring that priorities are met for a variety of needs. We are the consummate jugglers. Anne Morrow Lindbergh said, "What a circus act we women perform every day of our lives. It puts the trapeze artist to shame."

The history of women assuming multiple roles and meeting the needs of many people from diverse populations provided strong role models for flexibly responding to varying requests. The organizational skills and flexibility needed to cope with today's demands are hallmarks of female behaviors. Current societal demands require the ability to move seamlessly from task to task.

Women pay attention to details and shift easily from one task to the next. Women check off items on their many lists and then create a new list. We excel at accomplishing our projects, while ensuring nothing slips through the cracks. We master details and savor the enjoyment of the completed task.

The mere act of handling assignments from various people in our lives has conditioned us to tolerate interruptions with minimal resent-ment. As a woman, you have the ability to sustain an interruption and return to the task at hand. The talent of being "interruption proof" allows you the flexibility to respond to the changing demands of both your work and home environment.

Managing multiple priorities is a necessary part of the business world. As the intensity of communication increases — through mail, email, smart phones, faxes, and personal interactions — women have to sort quickly through the burgeoning requests, all the while prioritizing and keeping the overall purpose in sight. Past experiences have turned us into multitasking wizards able to balance and satisfy multiple projects — key skills for today's business world.

Change Tolerant

Women always have needed to quickly change focus to respond to demands from different sources. The ability to balance priorities requires us to be sufficiently flexible to move quickly between different tasks. Add to this our ability to tolerate ambiguity. Clear direction isn't always available, and women rarely have the time or luxury to completely and unambiguously understand all relationships formed by any negotiation or solution. In the big picture, you want to make the world a better place for those who follow and your children. Your concern with world welfare causes you to have a global focus, which is well suited to today's economy. Women are visionary leaders, because they want to make a difference, not only for their organization, but for the world at large.

Integrators

Women, with their antennae reaching in many directions to gather data, develop a momentum to create consensus. Our behavioral momentum to reach a consensus fosters integration. We have a minimal tolerance for fragmentation and consistently coach our employees to develop an integrated perspective.

As a woman, you possess a psychological perspective to create webs of inclusion. You enjoy the mutuality of relationships. As a result, you integrate multiple resources to achieve your project's objectives. You maintain an openness to integrate new people, new ideas, and new approaches.

Not only do you integrate on the macro level, you integrate on the micro level. Your management style is to consider both personal and business variables in using the talents of your work team. The consideration you demonstrate to your employees in understanding them as individuals builds strong loyalty. Your respect for their contributions and your integration of their ideas into projects energizes them. Loyalty and productive energy are valuable assets for all work environments.

Tap Your Talents

This chapter highlights just a few of the ways women contribute to the workplace. Recognize your talents are numerous. Now, bring your unique talents to the table with a sense of assurance, using your Positive Power. Research is clear: Women's collaborative approaches and team leadership style have already begun to transform the workplace. As you negotiate your next raise, as you develop your strategic career plan, as you establish your goals, do not doubt for a nanosecond the talent you bring to your company! For too long, women have allowed themselves to be held back by self-doubt, self-questioning, and feelings of powerlessness. The data is clear — your unique talents can only catapult you to limitless success.

Combining your recognition of your talents with your new Positive Power skills provides a wonderful synergy for an outstanding quality of life and success. As you activate and "power up," you create multiple possibilities both personally and professionally.

Positive Power Tools Summary

Power Robber Counter Thoughts

If I am accommodating and pleasing, I will have many friends and a rewarding life.
- Someone being disappointed in me is not a life or death matter.
- Making decisions in the professional arena should be weighed in professional not personal terms.
- My happiness comes from within. I do not depend on approval from the outside world to make me happy.
- I am committed to a program of self-approval and self-affirmation on a daily basis.
- Others' opinions do not define me. If they do not like me or if they reject me, this does not diminish me in any way; this is only their opinion.
- Being liked and approved by others is favorable, but not necessary for professional and personal success.
- I can make choices that nurture me to reach my potential.

I want to do it right and not make mistakes.
- Perfection is an unrealistic expectation.
- Avoiding failure is paralyzing.
- I want to be conscientious, not perfect.
- I can only make the best decision at the time.
- I can be myself; I do not have to prove myself.
- I see my mistakes as temporary setbacks and learning opportunities.

I want to avoid upsetting others.
- I am not responsible for the feelings of others.
- Someone liking me is not as important as me liking myself.
- There is more than one way of looking at things, and I am entitled to my opinion.

- I have the right to express annoyances and do not have to escalate into anger.
- I can engage in constructive negotiation and not damage my relationships.
- I need to give feedback on problem behaviors so adjustments can be made.

If there is a problem, it is my fault.
- Problems are a natural part of living.
- I do the best I can; I need to monitor my guilt.
- I cannot change the past, I can only move on.
- I am responsible for my own behaviors.
- I cannot control the full outcome.
- Worry is nonproductive.

I need to be polite and not make direct requests.
- I can be courteous without being deferentially polite.
- Making requests does not require asking permission.
- Indirectness slows the progress of my goals.
- Direct requests are necessary for effective communication.
- Clarity in communication brings you closer to your goals.

I want others to like me.
- It is important to develop my own goals based on my values and priorities.
- I am respectful of others, but do not let them control my actions.
- I determine my own actions.
- Popularity is fleeting. Living an authentic life is permanent.
- The most important perception is the perception I have of myself.
- No one has the power to diminish my personal value.

I need to obey the rules.
- Rules cannot cover all circumstances.
- Rules need to be bent to fit the situation.

- Rules can be creatively applied.
- For every rule, there is an exception.

I need to treat everyone equally.
- Different people add differently to my life.
- Different circumstances need to be responded to with different behaviors.
- Life is not a neat process where everything can be given out in equal measure.
- Each situation must be evaluated independently with consideration of many variables.

I must keep the peace and not make waves.
- Having a different opinion is not adversarial.
- I can be considerate and respectful while still expressing my opinion.
- Expressing an opinion and taking a stand is necessary for women's wisdom to have an impact.
- All conflict is not to be avoided.
- Varying perspectives from women and men enhance decisions.

I must wait to be recognized for my achievements.
- I am responsible for commendable work and creating opportunities for acknowledgement.
- Bragging and acknowledging are two different behaviors.
- I strive to accept compliments without minimizing behaviors.
- I am committed to appropriately accepting credit and giving credit to others.

Positive Power Affirmations

I need to set limits and engage in adequate self-care.
- As I engage in adequate self-care, I maintain my energy for my life's tasks.
- I focus on my own internal gauge of self-care and comfort.

- I listen to my inner voice and balance my life.
- I want to be considerate of others, not consumed by others.
- A disappointment is not a disaster.
- Healthy-selfish behaviors allow me to be considerate of others and myself.
- Living healthy-selfish results in a balanced life.

I welcome mistakes as an indicator I am pushing my limits and being all I can be.
- I will engage in self-correction, not self-condemnation.
- Corrective input from others is to be welcomed, not defended.
- A mistake is an opportunity to learn.
- If there is a mistake, I will be gentle and tolerant with myself.
- Mistakes are part of my humanity, and I refuse to condemn myself for any shortcomings or mistakes.
- As a seeker of excellence, not a perfectionist, I am open to direction and constructive criticism.

I seek respect of others and recognize some people will be uncomfortable around me.
- Being respected by others is more important than being liked.
- Disagreements are a healthy exchange of different viewpoints.
- Constructive conflict can strengthen relationships.
- As a female, I need to be tolerant of male colleagues who are still adjusting to changes in the workforce.
- My goal is to be effective and productive.

I need to engage in positive self-talk and monitor over-responsibility.
- Remember the wisdom of Eleanor Roosevelt: No one can make you feel inferior without your consent.
- I am a worthwhile person.
- I can do anything I set my mind to.
- I recognize that my thoughts create my feelings.
- I affirm myself daily.

- I am the captain of my own cheerleading team.
- I am committed to liking myself and accepting myself.
- Attitude is important, and I see the glass as half full.
- I engage in daily "mindercise" and physical exercise.

I need to ask for what I want to reach my goals.
- People cannot read my mind; I must say what I want.
- I want to maximize the possibility of reaching my goals.
- I am responsible for getting what I need.
- If I ask directly, I increase the possibility of having my request fulfilled.
- By asking clearly and directly, I am an effective communicator.
- I need to consistently plan and reassess my life goals.
- I seize opportunities to reach my goals.

I am centered and value myself.
- My relationships are only a portion of my life, and I am independently capable.
- I can set meaningful goals that give direction to my life.
- I can choose what I want and go after it.
- I can ask for help when I need it.
- I can be flexible and persistent in pursuing my goals.
- I recognize and develop my talents.

I need to understand the rules and be flexible.
- I recognize that rules may become outdated.
- I respect the rules but know they need to be challenged at times.
- I value my ability to be flexible and conduct a situational analysis.
- I have the ability to question rules and make needed changes.
- People are more important than rules.
- I consider both written and unwritten rules in my decision-making.
- I choose to be a change agent and establish new rules, when appropriate.

I need to be discriminating in my interactions with others.
- I must carefully invest my time.

- I must wisely invest my physical and emotional energies.
- I make discriminating use of time and energy to increase my quality of living.
- By being discriminating, I have adequate time for self-care.
- I reserve my time for people who are most important to me.
- I develop alliances that benefit me.

I want to make waves and be a change catalyst.
- I have a unique perspective that needs to be expressed.
- Being a change agent adds meaning to my life.
- I enjoy the challenge of moving an organization in new directions.
- As a change agent, I maintain critical alliances.
- Taking initiative is crucial to reaching my goals.
- Taking initiative allows me to shape the organization toward my vision.

I acknowledge my accomplishments and seek appropriate recognition.
- Acknowledgments are not boasting.
- Recognition creates new opportunities.
- "Tooting my own horn" is necessary for advancement.
- When I acknowledge my achievements, I also can acknowledge others' achievements and strengthen my alliances.
- I seek opportunities to be recognized.
- I recognize that by being acknowledged I position myself as a leader.

LeanIn.org

How to Continue Building Your Positive Power Skills

There is a special synergy between Sheryl Sandberg's book *Lean In: Women, Work, and the Will to Lead* and our book *Power Up: Charging Up for a Fuller Life.* Both books encourage women to pursue their ambitions and change the conversation from what we can't do to what we can do. The *Power Up* authors believe Positive Power is the key to "leaning in" and being successful personally and professionally.

LeanIn.org is an outstanding resource for our readers. It provides a forum where women can continue to develop their Positive Power skills and supports them in three essential ways:

1. *Community:* LeanIn.org wants all women to have the confidence and know-how to achieve their goals. The best place to start is with an active and supportive community. That's why each day the website encourages an open exchange of ideas and information, as well as shares Lean In stories.
2. *Education:* LeanIn.org offers a growing library of free online lectures on relevant topics such as leadership and communication.
3. *Circles:* Small groups of women who meet monthly to encourage and support each other in an atmosphere of confidentiality and trust.

Elizabeth Hyatt is a member of LeanIn.org and has created a Lean In Circle. Veronica Ruiz-Ashwal, LMHC, MBA, and Priscilla V. Marotta, Ph.D., are frequent visitors to the circle. We urge you to join their Circle and continue the important power conversations initiated by *Power Up.*

About the Authors

Veronica Ruiz-Ashwal, LMHC, MBA

Veronica Ruiz-Ashwal is the owner and president of the Center of Psychological Effectiveness, Inc., an outpatient behavioral health practice in Plantation, Florida. The Center provides cognitive-behavioral services, offering "solutions…not talk" for difficult times and life planning. She completed her graduate degrees in Mental Health Counseling and her MBA at the Miami campus of Carlos Albizu University.

Ms. Ruiz-Ashwal has held a number of leadership positions in the field. Since 2003, she has worked in several mental health positions, including executive director of a behavioral modification program and the principal of an alternative military academy for troubled youth. She has overseen utilization quality assurance, case management, and alternative to residential treatment programs in Miami-Dade and Broward counties. She has been involved in the Miami Chamber of Commerce, was a journalist for the Weston Newspaper, and currently is an active member of Mujeres Latinas in Broward County.

Over the course of her career, Ms. Ruiz-Ashwal has proven to be effective in setting up innovative systems in numerous facilities. She is a nationally awarded winner of Latino Who's Who in 2012, and a leader in the community service spectrum. Today, she is committed to providing a safe, nurturing environment for her patients and serve as a positive role model for future generations. She is the proud mother of Joseph Ashwal and wife of Ira Ashwal.

Elizabeth Hyatt

Elizabeth Hyatt is a student at the University of Florida, Gainesville, in a combined degree program, which will result in a bachelor's in political science and a master's in political campaigning. Her passion for politics resulted in numerous professional opportunities, including working for the United States House of Representatives, Florida Senate, Florida House, Rock the Vote, and several political campaigns.

In conjunction with her many political commitments, Ms. Hyatt began interning at the Center of Psychological Effectiveness, Inc., in her sophomore year of high school. Her internship evolved into serving as editor of the Center's monthly newsletter and director of social media.

Ms. Hyatt is recognized as one of the University of Florida's campus leaders, serving as a Florida Cicerone, Reitz Union Scholar, and Bob Graham Civic Scholar. Also a passionate advocate in the cancer community, she serves on the University of Florida's Camp Kesem Board of Directors, Camp Kesem's National Student Panel and lobbied with One Voice Against Cancer (OVAC) to Congress on behalf of LIVESTRONG in Washington, D.C. Ms. Hyatt will graduate with her master's in May 2015.

Priscilla V. Marotta, Ph.D.

Nationally recognized psychologist, Priscilla V. Marotta, Ph.D., is an executive coach, therapist, professional speaker, trainer, and consultant. Her treatment philosophy is "solutions....not talk." Dr. Marotta was founder of the behavioral health practice now known as the Center of Psychological Effectiveness in 1990.

Her specialties include dual career couples, women in leadership, women's issues, mood disorders, and trauma. Presently, she serves on the Florida Psychological Association Committee for a "Psychologically Healthy Workplace". This is an initiative both in Florida and on the national level with the American Psychological Association. She has been the recipient of numerous awards, including Florida's Psychological Association's "What a Woman Award" for her contributions to the psychology of women, 100 Most Outstanding Women in Broward County, Millennium Medal of Honor, International Who's Who of Professionals, The World's Who's Who of Professional and Business Women, The Twentieth Century Award for Achievement, and Notable American Women.

In 2014, Dr. Marotta celebrates twenty-five years of business in a group practice, mentoring many licensed therapists over a quarter of a century. Dr. Marotta is an active member of the Women's Executive Club and Florida Psychological Association. She enjoys her outpatient practice and being a catalyst for change in her patients' lives. She is the proud mother of attorney Christopher Fiore Marotta and wife of Robert E. MacDonald.

Center
Of
Psychological
Effectiveness

(800) 714 - COPE (2673)
SolutionsNotTalk.com

The **Center of Psychological Effectiveness** is an outpatient behavioral health practice in Plantation (west of Fort Lauderdale), Fla. In 2014, the Center celebrates a significant milestone: 25 years of being a positive catalyst in clients' lives.

The licensed cognitive-behavior therapists at the Center of Psychological Effectiveness specialize in depression, relationships, hypnosis, trauma, anxiety, addictions, coping with aging, parenting skills, and life changes. They provide clinical interventions as well as life coaching and are highly skilled at helping clients **cope with life**.

Cognitive-behavior therapy (CBT) research consistently demonstrates high outcomes for clients. CBT therapists teach life tools so you can **live a life you love.** As life becomes more complicated, relief from stress is critical. Mobilizing to reach life goals becomes essential. And, oftentimes that requires a guide. We use the services of financial planners, why wouldn't we invest in "life planning" as well?

The Center's multidisciplinary treatment team offers cost-effective, solution-focused services, and a **free insurance benefit check** prior to treatment. Visit our website SolutionsNotTalk.com to sign up for our complimentary newsletter and review our comprehensive services.

Writing that Bears Results

I was the kid in the neighborhood who checked out the maximum number of books allowed from the library each week. Every day you could find me in the giant ficus tree in my yard nibbling on a sandwich but devouring the book.

My fascination with words never waned. I earned a degree in English from the University of Florida — at a time when men outnumbered women ten to one. (That's certainly changed!) I've always instinctively understood the *power* of words — to move us, motivate us, inspire us, empower us. That's why when Dr. Marotta asked me to edit **Power Up,** I responded with one of my favorite words: Absolutely!

What started out as just another assignment turned into an eye-opener as well as an affirmation. I was able to identify the power robber messages instilled in childhood that I fall for — even today. But, I also discovered how many Positive Power tools have become second nature to me. The realization that stances I took professionally, when I was twenty-something, left legacies for women like Veronica Ruiz-Ashwal and Elizabeth Hyatt is powerful!

Dee Moustakas, President
Kodiak Communications, Inc.
Writing. Editing. Proofreading.
Dee@KodiakCommunications.com

Women of Wisdom, Inc.

Women of Wisdom, Inc., is delighted to be the "official" publisher of *Power Up: Charging Up for a Fuller Life!* by Priscilla V. Marotta, Ph.D., Veronica Ruiz-Ashwal, LMHC, MBA, and Elizabeth Hyatt. As a company that specializes in publishing books and producing social media campaigns by, for, and about women, we have a strong commitment to "representing books women love, learn from, and lend to others." These components make up the mission of Women of Wisdom Publishing, a company founded by a woman, run by women, and supported by women.

The words, women of wisdom, often make people think of "women of power" and "women of influence." The very term, wisdom (according to Dictionary.com) means: the quality or state of being wise; knowledge of what is true or right coupled with just judgment as to action; sagacity, discernment, or insight.

Wisdom, in my humble opinion, is so much more than that. It is learning to recognize our own strengths and trust our instincts, something most women of wisdom garner intellectually and emotionally from years of experience.

In fact, that is exactly how Women of Wisdom, Inc., came to be. It was created by an experienced and knowledgeable woman who was seeking female peers with whom she could identify, network, and grow with — both personally and professionally. That woman is Priscilla Marotta, one of the authors of this book. She has been, and still is, a role model and mentor to many women. As a woman of wisdom, she recognized early on that her purpose in life was to help other women create and sustain lives of meaning, purpose, and success. Thank you Dr. Marotta for being that woman for me.

At 19, I adopted the mantra to "live, learn, and pass it on." Women of Wisdom, Inc., is an extension of that. Our goal is to assist women in creating a platform to share the knowledge and skills they have learned through the years. Often hard earned through formal education and, perhaps more important, through living and experiencing life, wisdom is more meaningful when shared with others.

Representing both fiction and nonfiction works, Women of Wisdom, Inc., strives to showcase books that open doors to living richer, fuller lives. Our first book, *Power and Wisdom: The New Path for Women*, laid the groundwork. This book builds on it.

Enjoy *Power Up: Charging Up for a Fuller Life!* And, if you're an aspiring writer interested in publishing your book (whether first, or next), please keep Women of Wisdom, Inc., in mind. You can find us online at **WomenofWisdom.com** or call **954-625-6606.**

Heidi Richards Mooney, Publisher & President
Women of Wisdom, Inc.
WE Magazine for Women

Bibliography

Introduction

Allen, Tammy. "Career Benefits Associated with Mentoring for Protégés: A Meta Analysis", *Journal of Applied Psychology*, 89, No. 1. January 2004.

Kristof, Nicholas. "Women Hurting Women" *New York Times*, September 29, 2012.

Goux, Darshan. "Millennials in the Workplace," *Bentley University Center for Women and Business*, 17-25, 2012.

Jones, Bernie (ed). *Women Who Opt Out: The Debate over Working Mothers and Work-Family Balance*, New York University Press, 2012.

Marotta, Priscilla. *Power and Wisdom: The New Path for Women*. Women of Wisdom, Fla., 1999.

Sandberg, Sheryl. *Lean In: Women, Work, and the Will to Lead*. New York: Alfred A. Knopf, 2013.

Tremain, Rose, GoodReads.com

Williams, Jean and Boushey, Heather. 'The Three Faces of Work-Family Conflict: the Poor, the Professionals, and the Missing Middle.' *Center for American Progress and Center for Worklife Law*, January 2010.

Chapter 1

Aburdene, Patricia, Naisbitt, John. *Megatrends for Women: From Liberation to Leadership.* New York: Ballantine Books, 24, 1992.

Barsh, J., Cranston, S., & Lewis, G. *How Remarkable Women Lead: The Breakthrough Model for Work and Life.* New York: Crown Business, 2011.

Brown, E., Haygood, M., & McLena, R. *The Little Black Book of Success: Laws of Leadership for Black Women.* New York: One World Books, 2010.

Cummings, Nicholas. *Saving Health Dollars through Psychological Service.* May 1985.

Friedan, Betty. *The Feminine Mystique.* New York: W.W. Norton & Co., Inc., 1963.

Martz, Sandra Haldeman. *At Our Core: Women Writing About Power.* Watsonville, Calif.: Paper-Mache Press, 1998.

Offermann, Lynn R. "The Development and Validation of the Power Apprehension Scale." *Educational and Psychological Measurement,* 46, 437-441, 1986.

Offermann, Lynn R., & Beil, Cheryl. "Achievement Styles of Women Leaders and Their Peers." *Psychology of Women Quarterly,* 16:1, 53, 1992.

Miller, Cynthia L. & Cummins, A. Gaye. "An Examination of Women's Perspectives on Power." *Psychology of Women Quarterly,* 16:4, 415-428, 1992.

Sandberg, Sheryl. *Lean In: Women, Work, and the Will to Lead.* New York: Alfred A. Knopf, 2013.

Steinem, Gloria. "A Community of Women" in Helene Lerner-Robbins, ed., *Our Power As Women: The Wisdom and Strategies of Highly Successful Women.* Berkeley, Calif.: 16-20, 1996.

Warner, Carolyn. *The Last Word.* Englewood Cliffs, N.J.: Prentice Hall, 4, 47, 75, 263, 1992.

Webster's New Universal Unabridged Dictionary. New York: Random House Value Publishing Inc., 1516, 1996.

Wolf, Naomi. *Fire With Fire: The New Female Power and How to Use It.* New York: Random House, Inc., preface, 1993.

Chapter 2

Austin, D. Fit and Fabulous After 40: A 5-Part Program for Turning Back the Clock. New York: Broadway Books, 2002.

Baruch, Grace K. Reflections on Guilt, Women, and Gender. Wellesley College, Center for Research on Women, Working Paper Series 176, 1998.

Beaman, Robyn, Wheldall, Kevin & Kemp, Carol. "Differential Teacher Attention to Boys and Girls in the Classroom" Educational Review, 58, No. 3, 339-366, 2006.

Bem, Sandra Lipsitz. The Lenses of Gender: Transforming the Debate on Sexual Inequality. New Haven, Conn.: Yale University Press, 1993.

Brokaw, S. Fortytude: Making the Next Decades the Best Years of Life — Through the 40s, 50s, 60s. New York: Voice, 2011.

Clegg, Eileen M., & Swartz, Susan. Goodbye Good Girl. Oakland, Calif.: New Harbinger Publications, Inc., 3, 1997.

Cook, Ellen Piel. Women, Relationships, and Power. Alexandria, Va.: American Counseling Association, 1993.

Davidson, Marilyn J., & Cooper, Cary L. Shattering the Glass Ceiling: The Woman Manager. London: Paul Chapman Publishing Ltd., 1992.

DeAngelis, Tori. "Stereotypes Still Stymie Female Managers." American Psychological Association Monitor. 41-42, August 1997.

Elliott, Miriam & Meltsner, Susan. The Perfectionist Predicament. New York: William Morrow and Company, Inc., 1991

Epstein, Gene. Low Ceiling: How women are held back by sexism at work and child-rearing duties at home. Barron's Periodical, 35-40, December 1, 1997.

Forbes, Moira. "Hilary Clinton: Why Women Must 'Dare to Compete' in Politics", Forbes. June 26, 2013.

Goudreau, Jenna. "World's Most Powerful Women in Politics." Forbes, August 29, 2001.

Gaskill, Stephen. "A Solid Investment: Making Full Use of the Nation's Human Capital." Recommendations of the Federal Glass Ceiling

Commission. Washington, D.C: U.S. Government Printing Office, November 1995.

Heilman, Madeline and Okimoto. "Why are Women Penalized for Success at Male Task" Journal of Applied Psychology, 92. No. 1, 2007.

Howard, Carolyn "The New Class of Female CEO's" Forbes, August 22, 2012.

Maglin, Nan Bauer & Perry, Donna (eds.). Bad Girls/Good Girls: Women, Sex, and Power in the Nineties. New Brunswick, N.J.: Rutgers University Press, 1996.

Marotta, Priscilla. Power and Wisdom: The New Path for Women. Women of Wisdom, Fla., 1999.

Mindell, Phyllis. A Woman's Guide to the Language of Success: Communicating with Confidence and Power. Paramus, N.J.: Prentice Hall, 37, 1995.

Paglia, Camille. Vamps and Tramps. New York: Vintage Books, ix, 1994.

Powell, Gary N., & Butterfield, D. Anthony. "Investigating the 'Glass Ceiling' Phenomenon: An Empirical Study of Actual Promotions to Top Management." Academy of Management Journal, 37:1, 68-86, 1994.

Scheinholtz, Debra F., ed. Cracking the Glass Ceiling: Strategies for Success. New York: Catalyst, 1994.

Warner, Carolyn. The Last Word. Englewood Cliffs, N.J.: Prentice Hall, 93, 180, 1992.

Chapter 3

Danaher, Kelly & Crandell, Christian, "Stereotype threat in Applied Settings Reexamined" Journal of Applied Social Psychology. 38, No. 6, 1639-1655, 2008.

DeAngelis, Tori. "Stereotypes Still Stymie Female Managers." American Psychological Association Monitor. 41-42, August 1997.

Gilberd, Pamela Boucher. The Eleven Commandments of Wildly Successful Women. New York: Macmillan Spectrum, 1996.

Ely, Robyn & Rhode, Deborah, "Women and Leadership: Defining the Challenges," Handbook of Leadership Theory and Practioners ed.

Nitrin Nohira, and Rakesh Khurana C Boston: Harvard Business School Publishing, 2010.

Glick, Peter & Fisker, Susan, "The Ambivalent Sexism Inventory: Differentiating Hostile and Benevolent Sexism." Journal of Personality and Social Psychology, 70 No. 3, 491-512, 1996.

Heilman, Madeline. "Description and Prescription: How Gender Stereotypes Prevent Women's Ascent up the Organizational Ladder," Journal of Social Issues, 57, No. 4, 2001.

Heilman, Madeline E., Block, Caryn J., Martell, Richard F. "Sex Stereotypes: Do They Influence Perceptions of Managers?" in Nancy J. Struthers, ed., Gender in the Workplace [special issue], Journal of Social Behavior and Personality 10:36, 237-52. Corte Madera, Calif.: Select Press, 1995.

Hewlett, Sylvia Ann & Luce, Carolyn Boet "Off Ramps and On Ramps: Keeping Talented Women on the Road to Success", Harvard Business Review, 83, No. 3, 2005.

O'Gorman, Patricia. Dancing Backwards in High Heels. Center City, Minn: Hazelden Education Materials, 1994.

Rubin, Harriet. The Princessa: Machiavelli for Women. New York: Doubleday, 1997.

Sandberg, Sheryl. Lean In: Women, Work, and the Will to Lead. New York: Alfred A. Knopf, 2013.

U.S. Department of Labor, Bureau of Labor Statistics, 2010.

U.S. Department of Education, National Center for Education Statistics. Digest of Education Statistics, 2011 (NCES 2012-001).

Warner, Carolyn. The Last Word. Englewood Cliffs, N.J.: Prentice Hall, 93, 180, 1992.

Chapter 4

Belenky, Mary Field, Clinchy, Blythe McVicker, Goldberger, Nancy Rule, Tarule, & Jill Mattuck. Women's Ways of Knowing: The Development of Self, Voice, and Mind. New York: Basic Books, Inc., 1997.

Bem, Sandra Lipsitz. The Lenses of Gender: Transforming the Debate on Sexual Inequality. New Haven, Conn.: Yale University Press, 1993.

Boles, Janet K., & Hoeveler, Diane Long. From the Goddess to the Glass Ceiling: A Dictionary of Feminism. Lanham, Md.: Madison Books, 1996.

Gilligan, C. In a Different Voice: Psychological Theory and Women's Development. Harvard University Press, 1993.

Helgesen, Sally. The Female Advantage. New York: Doubleday, 1990.

Lerner-Robbins, Helene. *Our Power as Women: The Wisdom and Strategies of Highly Successful Women.* Berkeley, Calif.: Conari Press, 1996.

Lorber, Judith V. Paradoxes of Gender. New Haven. Conn.: Yale University Press, 1994.

Matlin, M. The Psychology of Women. Belmont, Calif.: Cengage Learning, 2011.

Miller, Jean Baker. *The Healing Connection: How Women Form Relationships in Therapy and in Life.* Boston, Mass.: Beacon Press, 1998.

Warner, Carolyn. The Last Word. Englewood Cliffs, N.J.: Prentice Hall, 4, 47, 75, 263, 1992.

Winfrey, Oprah. Wesleyan University Commencement Address, Connecticut, 1998.

Chapter 5

Amanatullah, Emily, & Morris, Michael. "Negotiating Gender Rules: Gender Differences in Assertive Negotiating Are Mediated by Women's Fear of Backlash and Attenuated when Negotiating on Behalf of Others." Journal of Personality and Social Psychology, 98, No. 2, 256-257, 2010.

Davis, Shirley. "For women, asking for a raise is damned if you do or don't", CNBC.com: November 27, 2013.

Lyness, Karen & Schrader, "Moving Ahead of Just Moving? An Examination of Gender Differences in Senior Corporate Management Appointments," Gender & Organization Management 31, No. 6, 651-676, 2006.

Paglia, Camille. Vamps and Tramps. New York: Vintage Books, ix, 1994.

Steinem, Gloria. Moving Beyond Words. New York: Simon Schuster, Inc., 1994.

Tannen, Deborah. You Just Don't Understand: Women and Men in Conversation. New York: Ballantine Books, 1990.

Warner, Carolyn. The Last Word. Englewood Cliffs, N.J.: Prentice Hall, 93, 180, 1992.

Chapter 6

Denmark, Florence L. "Women, Leadership, and Empowerment." Psychology of Women Quarterly, 17:343-356, 1993.

Goss, Tracy. The Last Word on Power: Executive Re-Invention for Leaders Who Must Make the Impossible Happen. New York: Doubleday, 15, 1996.

Heatherington, etal, "Two Investigators of 'Female Modesty' in Achievement Situations", Sex Roles, 29, No. 11 & 12, 739-754, 1993.

Horner, Althea. The Wish for Power and the Fear of Having It. Northvale, N.J.: Jason Aronson, Inc., 1989.

Johnson, Maria and Helegson, Vicki. "Sex Differences in Response to Evaluative Feedback: A Field Study" Psychology of Women Quarterly, 26, No. 3, 242-281, 2002.

Miller, Cynthia L. & Cummins, A. Gaye. "An Examination of Women's Perspectives on Power." Psychology of Women Quarterly, 16:4, 415-428, 1992.

Warner, Carolyn. The Last Word. Englewood Cliffs, N.J.: Prentice Hall, 93, 180, 1992.

Chapter 7

Barnett, Chait Rosalind, "Women and Multiple Roles: Myths and Reality", Harvard Review of Psychology, 12, No. 3, 158-164, 2004.

Bem, Sandra Lipsitz. The Lenses of Gender: Transforming the Debate on Sexual Inequality. New Haven, Conn.: Yale University Press, 1993.

Brown, Elizabeth & Drekman, Amanda. "What Will I Be? Exploring Gender Differences in Near and Distant Possible Selves," Sex Roles, 63, No. 7 & 8, 2010.

Del Valle, Christina. "Glass Ceiling? What Glass Ceiling?" Businessweek, October 24, 1994.

Geary, David C. Male, Female: The Evolution of Human Sex Differences. Washington, D.C.: American Psychological Association, 1998.

Gilligan, Carol. In a Different Voice: Psychological Theory and Women's Development. Cambridge, Mass.: Harvard University Press, 1982.

Harrin, E. Overcoming Imposter Syndrome. New York: The Otobos Group, 2011.

Hassler, C. 20 Something 20 Everything. Novato, Calif.: New World Library, 2005.

Helgesen, Sally. The Female Advantage. New York: Doubleday, 1990.

Jordan, Judith V., Kaplan, Alexandra G., Miller, Jean Baker, Striver, Irene P., & Surrey, Janet L. Women's Growth and Connection: Writings From the Stone Center. New York: Guilford Press, 1991.

Jordan, Judith V. (ed.) Women's Growth in Diversity: More Writings From the Stone Center. New York: Guilford Press, 1997.

Lindbergh, Anne Morrow. Gift from the Sea. New York: Vintage Books, 1978.

Lips, Hilary, M. Woman, Men, and Power. Mountain View, Calif.: Mayfield Publishing Co., 1991.

Moir, A., & Jessel, D. Brain Sex: The Real Difference Between Men and Women. New York: Dell Publishing, 1992.

Rosen, Hana. The End of Men: And the Rise of Women. New York: Riverhead Books, 2012.

Rosener, Judy B. *America's Competitive Secret: Women Managers*. New York: Oxford University Press, 1995.

Rubin, Harriet. The Princessa: Machiavelli for Women. New York: Bantam Doubleday Dell Publishing Group, Inc., 21, 1997.

30 years later, is feminism dead? NBC News, February 8, 2005.

Warner, Carolyn. The Last Word. Englewood Cliffs, N.J.: Prentice Hall, 93, 180, 1992.

Wilson, Marie. Closing the Leadership Gap: Add Women Change Everything. New York: Penguin, 2007.

Index

www.ingramcontent.com/pod-product-compliance
Lightning Source LLC
Chambersburg PA
CBHW021430170526
45164CB00001B/168

www.ingramcontent.com/pod-product-compliance
Lightning Source LLC
Chambersburg PA
CBHW021420170526
45164CB00001B/28